Florence

to

Trieste

Jacques Casanova de Seingalt

[ZHINGOORA BOOKS]

CHAPTER XVIII

Madame Denis—Dedini—Zanovitch—Zen—I Am Obliged to Leave—I Arrive at Bologna—General Albergati

Without speaking at any length I asked the young grand duke to give me an asylum in his dominions for as long as I might care to stay. I anticipated any questions he might have asked by telling him the reasons which had made me an exile from my native land.

"As to my necessities," I added, "I shall ask for help of no one; I have sufficient funds to ensure my independence. I think of devoting the whole of my time to study."

"So long as your conduct is good," he replied, "the laws guarantee your freedom; but I am glad you have applied to me. Whom do you know in Florence?"

"Ten years ago, my lord, I had some distinguished acquaintances here; but now I propose to live in retirement, and do not intend renewing any old friendships."

Such was my conversation with the young sovereign, and after his assurances I concluded that no one would molest me.

My adventures in Tuscany the years before were in all probability forgotten, or almost forgotten, as the new Government had nothing in common with the old.

After my interview with the grand duke I went to a bookseller's shop and ordered some books. A gentleman in the shop, hearing me making enquiries about Greek works, accosted me, and we got on well together. I told him I was working at a translation of the "Iliad," and in return he informed me that he was making a collection of Greek epigrams, which he wished to publish in Greek and Italian. I told him I should like to see this work, whereupon he asked me where I lived. I told him, learnt his name and address, and called on him the next day. He returned the visit, and we became fast friends, though we never either walked or ate together.

This worthy Florentine was named (or is named, if he be still alive)
Everard de Medici.

I was very comfortable with Allegranti; I had the quiet so necessary to literary labours, but nevertheless I made up my mind to change my lodging. Magdalena, my landlord's niece, was so clever and charming, though but a child, that she continually disturbed my studies. She came into my room, wished me good day, asked me what kind of a night I had spent, if I wanted anything, and the sight of her grace and beauty and the sound of her voice so ravished me, that I determined to seek safety in flight.

A few years later Magdalena became a famous musician.

After leaving Allegranti I took rooms in a tradesman's house; his wife was ugly, and he had no pretty daughters or seductive nieces. There I lived for three weeks like Lafontaine's rat, very discreetly.

About the same time, Count Stratico arrived at Florence with his pupil, the Chevalier Morosini, who was then eighteen. I could not avoid calling on Stratico. He had broken his leg some time before and was still unable to go out with his pupil, who had all the vices and none of the virtues of youth. Consequently, Stratico was always afraid of something happening to him, and he begged me to make myself his companion, and even to share his pleasures, so that he might not go into bad company and dangerous houses alone and undefended.

Thus my days of calm study vanished away. I had to partake in the debauchery of a young rake, and all out of pure sensibility.

The Chevalier Morosini was a thorough-paced profligate. He hated literature, good society, and the company of sensible people. His daily pleasures were furious riding, hard drinking, and hard dissipation with prostitutes, whom he sometimes almost killed.

This young nobleman paid a man for the sole service of getting him a woman or a girl every day.

During the two months which he passed in Florence I saved his life a score of times. I got very tired of my duty, but I felt bound to persevere.

He was liberal to the verge of recklessness, and would never allow me to pay for anything. Even here, however, disputes often arose between us; as he paid, he wanted me to eat, drink, and dissipate in the same measures as himself. However, I had my own way on most occasions, only giving in when it suited me to do so.

We went to see the opera at Lucca, and drought two of the dancers home to supper. As the chevalier was drunk as usual, he treated the woman he had chosen—a superb creature—very indifferently. The other was pretty enough, but I had done nothing serious with her, so I proceeded to avenge the beauty. She took me for the chevalier's father, and advised me to give him a better education.

After the chevalier was gone I betook myself to my studies again, but I supped every night with Madame Denis, who had formerly been a dancer in the King of Prussia's service, and had retired to Florence.

She was about my age, and therefore not young, but still she had sufficient remains of her beauty to inspire a tender passion; she did not look more than thirty. She was as fresh as a young girl, had excellent manners, and was extremely intelligent. Besides all these advantages, she had a comfortable apartment on the first floor of one of the largest cafes in Florence. In front of her room was a balcony where it was delicious to sit and enjoy the cool of the evening.

The reader may remember how I had become her friend at Berlin in 1764, and when we met again at Florence our old flames were rekindled.

The chief boarder in the house where she lived was Madame Brigonzi, whom I had met at Memel. This lady, who pretended that she had been my mistress twenty-five years before, often came into Madame Denis's rooms with an old lover of hers named Marquis Capponi.

He was an agreeable and well-educated man; and noticing that he seemed to enjoy my conversation I called on him, and he called on me, leaving his card as I was not at home.

I returned the visit, and he introduced me to his family and invited me to dinner. For the first time since I had come to Florence I dressed myself with elegance and wore my jewels.

At the Marquis Capponi's I made the acquaintance of Corilla's lover, the Marquis Gennori, who took me to a house where I met my fate. I fell in love with Madame a young widow, who had been spending a few months in Paris. This visit had added to her other attractions the charm of a good manner, which always counts for so much.

This unhappy love made the three months longer which I spent in Florence painful to me.

It was at the beginning of October, and about that time Count Medini arrived at Florence without a penny in his pocket, and without being able to pay his vetturino, who had arrested him.

The wretched man, who seemed to follow me wherever I went, had taken up his abode in the house of a poor Irishman.

I do not know how Medini found out that I was at Florence, but he wrote me a letter begging me to come and deliver him from the police, who besieged his room and talked of taking him to prison. He said he only wanted me to go bail for him, and protested that I should not run any risk, as he was sure of being able to pay in a few days.

My readers will be aware that I had good reason for not liking Medini, but in spite of our quarrel I could not despise his entreaty. I even felt inclined to become his surety, if he could prove his capability of paying the sum for which he had been arrested. I imagined that the sum must be a small one, and could not understand why the landlord did not answer for him. My surprise ceased, however, when I entered his room.

As soon as I appeared he ran to embrace me, begging me to forget the past, and to extract him from the painful position in which he found himself.

I cast a rapid glance over the room, and saw three trunks almost empty, their contents being scattered about the floor. There was his mistress, whom I knew, and who had her reasons for not liking me; her young sister, who wept; and her mother, who swore, and called Medini a rogue, saying that she would complain of him to the magistrate, and that she was not going to allow her dresses and her daughter's dresses to be seized for his debts.

I asked the landlord why he did not go bail, as he had these persons and their effects as security.

"The whole lot," he answered, "won't pay the vetturino, and the sooner they are out of my house the better I shall be pleased."

I was astonished, and could not understand how the bill could amount to more than the value of all the clothes I saw on the floor, so I asked the vetturino to tell me the extent of the debt.

He gave me a paper with Medini's signature; the amount was two hundred and forty crowns.

"How in the world," I exclaimed, "could he contract this enormous debt?"

I wondered no longer when the vetturino told me that he had served them for the last six weeks, having conducted the count and the three women from Rome to Leghorn, and from Leghorn to Pisa, and from Pisa to Florence, paying for their board all the way.

"The vetturino will never take me as bail for such an amount," I said to Medini, "and even if he would I should never be so foolish as to contract such a debt."

"Let me have a word with you in the next room," said he; "I will put the matter clearly before you."

"Certainly."

Two of the police would have prevented his going into the next room, on the plea that he might escape through the window, but I said I would be answerable for him.

Just then the poor vetturino came in and kissed my hand, saying that if I would go bail for the count he would let me have three months wherein to find the money.

As it happened it was the same man who had taken me to Rome with the Englishwoman who had been seduced by the actor L'Etoile. I told him to wait a moment.

Medini who was a great talker and a dreadful liar thought to persuade me by shewing me a number of open letters, commending him in pompous terms to the best houses in Florence. I read the letters, but I found no mention of money in them, and I told him as much.

"I know," said he, "but there is play going on in these houses, and I am sure of gaining immense sums."

"You may be aware that I have no confidence in your good luck."

"Then I have another resource."

"What is that?"

He shewed me a bundle of manuscript, which I found to be an excellent translation of Voltaire's "Henriade" into Italian verse. Tasso himself could not have done it better. He said he hoped to finish the poem at Florence, and to present it to the grand duke, who would be sure to make him a magnificent present, and to constitute him his favourite.

I would not undeceive him, but I laughed to myself, knowing that the grand duke only made a pretence of loving literature. A certain Abbe Fontaine, a clever man, amused him with a little natural history, the only science in which he took any interest. He preferred the worst prose to the best verse, not having sufficient intellect to enjoy the subtle charms of poetry. In reality he had only two passions—women and money.

After spending two wearisome hours with Medini, whose wit was great and his judgment small, after heartily repenting of having yielded to my curiosity and having paid him a visit, I said shortly that I could do nothing for him. Despair drives men crazy; as I was making for the door, he seized me by the collar.

He did not reflect in his dire extremity that he had no arms, that I was stronger than he, that I had twice drawn his blood, and that the police, the landlord, the vetturirco, and the servants, were in the next room. I was not coward enough to call for help; I caught hold of his neck with both hands and squeezed him till he was nearly choked. He had to let go at last, and then I took hold of his collar and asked him if he had gone mad.

I sent him against the wall, and opened the door and the police came in.

I told the vetturino that I would on no account be Medini's surety, or be answerable for him in any way.

Just as I was going out, he leapt forward crying that I must not abandon him.

I had opened the door, and the police, fearing he would escape, ran forward to get hold of him. Then began an interesting battle. Medini, who had no arms, and was only in his dressing-gown, proceeded to distribute kicks, cuffs, and blows amongst the four cowards, who had their swords at their sides, whilst I held the door to prevent the Irishman going out and calling for assistance.

Medini, whose nose was bleeding and his dress all torn, persisted in fighting till the four policemen let him alone. I liked his courage, and pitied him.

There was a moment's silence, and I asked his two liveried servants who were standing by me why they had not helped their master. One said he owed him six months' wages, and the other said he wanted to arrest him on his own account.

As Medini was endeavouring to staunch the blood in a basin of water, the vetturino told him that as I refused to be his surety he must go to prison.

I was moved by the scene that I had witnessed, and said to the vetturino,

"Give him a fortnight's respite, and if he escapes before the expiration of that term I will pay you."

He thought it over for a few moments, and then said,—

"Very good, sir, but I am not going to pay any legal expenses."

I enquired how much the costs amounted to, and paid them, laughing at the policemen's claim of damages for blows they had received.

Then the two rascally servants said that if I would not be surety in the same manner on their account, they would have Medini arrested. However, Medini called out to me to pay no attention to them whatever.

When I had given the vetturino his acknowledgment and paid the four or five crowns charged by the police, Medini told me that he had more to say to me; but I turned my back on him, and went home to dinner.

Two hours later one of his servants came to me and promised if I would give him six sequins to warn me if his master made any preparations for flight.

I told him drily that his zeal was useless to me, as I was quite sure that the count would pay all his debts within the term; and the next morning I wrote to Medini informing him of the step his servant had taken. He replied with a long letter full of thanks, in which he exerted all his eloquence to persuade me to repair his fortunes. I did not answer.

However, his good genius, who still protected him, brought a person to Florence who drew him out of the difficulty. This person was Premislas Zanovitch, who afterwards became as famous as his brother who cheated the Amsterdam merchants, and adopted the style of Prince Scanderbeck. I shall speak of him later on. Both these finished cheats came to a bad end.

Premislas Zanovitch was then at the happy age of twenty-five; he was the son of a gentleman of Budua, a town on the borders of Albania and Dalmatia, formerly subject to the Venetian Republic and now to the Grand Turk. In classic times it was known as Epirus.

Premislas was a young man of great intelligence, and after having studied at Venice, and contracted a Venetian taste for pleasures and enjoyments of all sorts, he could not make up his mind to return to Budua, where his only associates would be dull Sclavs—uneducated, unintellectual, coarse, and brutish. Consequently, when Premislas and his still more talented brother

Stephen were ordered by the Council of Ten to enjoy the vast sums they had gained at play in their own country, they resolved to become adventurers. One took the north and the other the south of Europe, and both cheated and duped whenever the opportunity for doing so presented itself.

I had seen Premislas when he was a child, and had already heard reports of a notable achievement of his. At Naples he had cheated the Chevalier de Morosini by persuading him to become his surety to the extent of six thousand ducats, and now he arrived in Florence in a handsome carriage, bringing his mistress with him, and having two tall lackeys and a valet in his service.

He took good apartments, hired a carriage, rented a box at the opera, had a skilled cook, and gave his mistress a lady-in-waiting. He then shewed himself at the best club, richly dressed, and covered with jewellery. He introduced himself under the name of Count Premislas Zanovitch.

There is a club in Florence devoted to the use of the nobility. Any stranger can go there without being introduced, but so much the worse for him if his appearance fails to indicate his right to be present. The Florentines are ice towards him, leave him alone, and behave in such a manner that the visit is seldom repeated. The club is at once decent and licentious, the papers are to be read there, games of all kinds are played, food and drink may be had, and even love is available, for ladies frequent the club.

Zanovitch did not wait to be spoken to, but made himself agreeable to everyone, and congratulated himself on mixing in such distinguished company, talked about Naples which he had just left, brought in his own name with great adroitness, played high, lost merrily, paid after pretending to forget all about his debts, and in short pleased everyone. I heard all this the next day from the Marquis Capponi, who said that someone had asked him if he knew me, whereat he answered that when I left Venice he was at college, but that he had often heard his father speak of me in very high terms. He knew both the Chevalier Morosini and Count Medini, and had a good deal to say in praise of the latter. The marquis asked me if I knew him, and I replied in the affirmative, without feeling it my duty to disclose certain circumstances which might not have been advantageous to him; and as Madame Denis seemed curious to make his acquaintance the Chevalier Puzzi promised to bring him to see her, which he did in the course of a few days.

I happened to be with Madame Denis when Puzzi presented Zanovitch, and I saw before me a fine-looking young men, who seemed by his confident manner to be sure of success in all his undertakings. He was not exactly handsome, but he had a perfect manner and an air of gaiety which seemed infectious, with a thorough knowledge of the laws of good society. He was by no means an egotist, and seemed never at a loss for something to talk about. I led the conversation to the subject of his country, and he gave me an amusing description of it, talking of his fief-part of which was within the domains of the sultan-as a place where gaiety was unknown, and where the most determined misanthrope would die of melancholy.

As soon as he heard my name he began speaking to me in a tone of the most delicate flattery. I saw the makings of a great adventurer in him, but I thought his luxury would prove the weak point in his cuirass. I thought him something like what I had been fifteen years ago, but as it seemed unlikely that he had my resources I could not help pitying him.

Zanovitch paid me a visit, and told me that Medini's position had excited his pity, and that he had therefore paid his debts.

I applauded his generosity, but I formed the conclusion that they had laid some plot between them, and that I should soon hear of the results of this new alliance.

I returned Zanovitch's call the next day. He was at table with his mistress, whom I should not have recognized if she had not pronounced my name directly she saw me.

As she had addressed me as Don Giacomo, I called her Donna Ippolita, but in a voice which indicated that I was not certain of her identity. She told me I was quite right.

I had supped with her at Naples in company with Lord Baltimore, and she was very pretty then.

Zanovitch asked me to dine with him the following day, and I should have thanked him and begged to be excused if Donna Ippolita had not pressed me to come. She assured me that I should find good company there, and that the cook would excel himself.

I felt rather curious to see the company, and with the idea of shewing Zanovitch that I was not likely to become a charge on his purse, I dressed myself magnificently once more.

As I had expected, I found Medini and his mistress there, with two foreign ladies and their attendant cavaliers, and a fine-looking and well-dressed Venetian, between thirty-five and forty, whom I would not have recognized if Zanovitch had not told me his name, Alois Zen.

"Zen was a patrician name, and I felt obliged to ask what titles I ought to give him.

"Such titles as one old friend gives another, though it is very possible you do not recollect me, as I was only ten years old when we saw each other last."

Zen then told me he was the son of the captain I had known when I was under arrest at St. Andrews.

"That's twenty-eight years ago; but I remember you, though you had not had the small-pox in those days."

I saw that he was annoyed by this remark, but it was his fault, as he had no business to say where he had known me, or who his father was.

He was the son of a noble Venetian—a good-for-nothing in every sense of the word.

When I met him at Florence he had just come from Madrid, where he had made a lot of money by holding a bank at faro in the house of the Venetian ambassador, Marco Zen.

I was glad to meet him, but I found out before the dinner was over that he was completely devoid of education and the manners of a gentleman; but he was well content with the one talent he possessed, namely, that of correcting the freaks of fortune at games of chance. I did not wait to see the onslaught of the cheats on the dupes, but took my leave while the table was being made ready.

Such was my life during the seven months which I spent at Florence.

After this dinner I never saw Zen, or Medini, or Zanovitch, except by chance in the public places.

Here I must recount some incidents which took place towards the middle of December.

Lord Lincoln, a young man of eighteen, fell in love with a Venetian dancer named Lamberti, who was a universal favourite. On every night when the opera was given the young Englishman might be seen going to her camerino, and everyone wondered why he did not visit her at her own house, where he would be certain of a good welcome, for he was English, and therefore rich, young, and handsome. I believe he was the only son of the Duke of Newcastle.

Zanovitch marked him down, and in a short time had become an intimate friend of the fair Lamberti. He then made up to Lord

Lincoln, and took him to the lady's house, as a polite man takes a friend to see his mistress.

Madame Lamberti, who was in collusion with the rascal, was not niggardly of her favours with the young Englishman. She received him every night to supper with Zanovitch and Zen, who had been presented by the Sclav, either because of his capital, or because Zanovitch was not so accomplished a cheat.

For the first few nights they took care to let the young nobleman win. As they played after supper, and Lord Lincoln followed the noble English custom of drinking till he did not know his right hand from his left, he was quite astonished on waking the next morning to find that luck had been as kind to him as love. The trap was baited, the young lord nibbled, and, as may be expected, was finally caught.

Zen won twelve thousand pounds of him, and Zanovitch lent him the money by installments of three and four hundred louis at a time, as the Englishman had promised his tutor not to play, on his word of honour.

Zanovitch won from Zen what Zen won from the lord, and so the game was kept up till the young pigeon had lost the enormous sum of twelve thousand guineas.

Lord Lincoln promised to pay three thousand guineas the next day, and signed three bills of exchange for three thousand guineas each, payable in six months, and drawn on his London banker.

I heard all about this from Lord Lincoln himself when we met at Bologna three months later.

The next morning the little gaming party was the talk of Florence. Sasso Sassi, the banker, had already paid Zanovitch six thousand sequins by my lord's orders.

Medini came to see me, furious at not having been asked to join the party, while I congratulated myself on my absence. My surprise may be imagined, when, a few days after, a person came up to my room, and ordered me to leave Florence in three days and Tuscany in a week.

I was petrified, and called to my landlord to witness the unrighteous order I had received.

It was December 28th. On the same date, three years before, I had received orders to leave Barcelona in three days.

I dressed hastily and went to the magistrate to enquire the reason for my exile, and on entering the room I found it was the same man who had ordered me to leave Florence eleven years before.

I asked him to give me his reasons, and he replied coldly that such was the will of his highness.

"But as his highness must have his reasons, it seems to me that I am within my rights in enquiring what they are."

"If you think so you had better betake yourself to the prince; I know nothing about it. He left yesterday for Pisa, where he will stay three days; you can go there."

"Will he pay for my journey?"

"I should doubt it, but you can see for yourself."

"I shall not go to Pisa, but I will write to his highness if you will promise to send on the letter."

"I will do so immediately, for it is my duty."

"Very good; you shall have the letter before noon tomorrow, and before day-break I shall be in the States of the Church."

"There's no need for you to hurry yourself."

"There is a very great hurry. I cannot breathe the air of a country where liberty is unknown and the sovereign breaks his word; that is what I am going to write to your master."

As I was going out I met Medini, who had come on the same business as myself.

I laughed, and informed him of the results of my interview, and how I had been told to go to Pisa.

"What! have you been expelled, too?"

"Yes."

"What have you done?"

"Nothing."

"Nor I. Let us go to Pisa."

"You can go if you like, but I shall leave Florence tonight."

When I got home I told my landlord to get me a carriage and to order four post-horses for nightfall, and I then wrote the following letter to the grand duke:

"My Lord; The thunder which Jove has placed in your hands is only for the guilty; in launching it at me you have done wrong. Seven months ago you promised that I should remain unmolested so long as I obeyed the laws. I have done so scrupulously, and your lordship has therefore broken your word. I am merely writing to you to let you know that I forgive you, and that I shall never give utterance to a word of complaint. Indeed I would willingly forget the injury you have done me, if it were not necessary that I should remember never to set foot in your realms again. The magistrate tells me that I can go and see you at Pisa, but I fear such a step would seem a hardy one to a prince, who should hear what a man has to say before he condemns him, and not afterwards.

"I am, etc."

When I had finished the letter I sent it to the magistrate, and then I began my packing.

I was sitting down to dinner when Medini came in cursing Zen and Zanovitch, whom he accused of being the authors of his misfortune, and of refusing to give him a hundred sequins, without which he could not possibly go.

"We are all going to Pisa," said he, "and cannot imagine why you do not come, too."

"Very good," I said, laughingly, "but please to leave me now as I have to do my packing."

As I expected, he wanted me to lend him some money, but on my giving him a direct refusal he went away.

After dinner I took leave of M. Medici and Madame Dennis, the latter of whom had heard the story already. She cursed the grand duke, saying she could not imagine how he could confound the innocent with the guilty. She informed me that Madame Lamberti had received orders to quit, as also a hunchbacked Venetian priest, who used to go and see the dancer but had never supped with her. In fact, there was a clean sweep of all the Venetians in Florence.

As I was returning home I met Lord Lincoln's governor; whom I had known at Lausanne eleven years before. I told him of what had happened to me through his hopeful pupil getting himself fleeced. He laughed, and told me that the grand duke had advised Lord Lincoln not to pay the money he had lost, to which the young man replied that if he were not to pay he should be dishonoured since the money he had lost had been lent to him.

In leaving Florence I was cured of an unhappy love which would doubtless have had fatal consequences if I had stayed on. I have spared my readers the painful story because I cannot recall it to my mind even now without being cut to the heart. The widow whom I loved, and to whom I was so weak as to disclose my feelings, only attached me to her triumphal car to humiliate me, for she disdained my love and myself. I persisted in my courtship, and nothing but my enforced absence would have cured me.

As yet I have not learnt the truth of the maxim that old age, especially when devoid of fortune, is not likely to prove attractive to youth.

I left Florence poorer by a hundred sequins than when I came there. I had lived with the most careful economy throughout the whole of my stay.

I stopped at the first stage within the Pope's dominions, and by the last day but one of the year I was settled at Bologna, at "St. Mark's Hotel."

My first visit was paid to Count Marulli, the Florentine charge d'affaires. I begged him to write and tell his master, that, out of gratitude for my banishment, I should never cease to sing his praises.

As the count had received a letter containing an account of the whole affair, he could not quite believe that I meant what I said.

"You may think what you like," I observed, "but if you knew all you would see that his highness has done me a very great service though quite unintentionally."

He promised to let his master know how I spoke of him.

On January 1st, 1772, I presented myself to Cardinal Braneaforte, the Pope's legate, whom I had known twenty years before at Paris, when he had been sent by Benedict XVI. with the holy swaddling clothes for the newly-born Duke of Burgundy. We had met at the Lodge of Freemasons, for the members of the sacred college were by no means afraid of their own anathemas. We had also some very pleasant little suppers with pretty sinners in company with Don Francesco Sensate and Count Ranucci. In short, the cardinal was a man of wit, and what is called a bon vivant.

"Oh, here you are!" cried he, when he saw me; "I was expecting you."

"How could you, my lord? Why should I have come to Bologna rather than to any other place?"

"For two reasons. In the first place because Bologna is better than many other places, and besides I flatter myself you thought of me. But you needn't say anything here about the life we led together when we were young men."

"It has always been a pleasant recollection to me."

"No doubt. Count Marulli told me yesterday that you spoke very highly of the grand duke, and you are quite right. You can talk to me in confidence; the walls of this room have no ears. How much did you get of the twelve thousand guineas?"

I told him the whole story, and shewed him a copy of the letter which I had written to the grand duke. He laughed, and said he was sorry I had been punished for nothing.

When he heard I thought of staying some months at Bologna he told me that I might reckon on perfect freedom, and that as soon as the matter ceased to become common talk he would give me open proof of his friendship.

After seeing the cardinal I resolved to continue at Bologna the kind of life that I had been leading at Florence. Bologna is the freest town in all Italy; commodities are cheap and good, and all the pleasures of life may be had there at a low price. The town is a fine one, and the streets are lined with arcades—a great comfort in so hot a place.

As to society, I did not trouble myself about it. I knew the Bolognese; the nobles are proud, rude, and violent; the lowest orders, known as the birichini, are worse than the lazzaroni of Naples, while the tradesmen and the middle classes are generally speaking worthy and respectable people. At Bologna, as at Naples, the two extremes of society are corrupt, while the middle classes are respectable, and the depository of virtue, talents, and learning.

However, my intention was to leave society alone, to pass my time in study, and to make the acquaintance of a few men of letters, who are easily accessible everywhere.

At Florence ignorance is the rule and learning the exception, while at Bologna the tincture of letters is almost universal. The university has thrice the usual number of professors; but they are all ill paid, and have to get their living out of the students, who are numerous. Printing is cheaper at Bologna than anywhere else, and though the Inquisition is established there the press is almost entirely free.

All the exiles from Florence reached Bologna four or five days after myself. Madame Lamberti only passed through on her way to Venice. Zanovitch and Zen stayed five or six days; but they were no longer in partnership, having quarreled over the sharing of the booty.

Zanovitch had refused to make one of Lord Lincoln's bills of exchange payable to Zen, because he did not wish to make himself liable in case the Englishman refused to pay. He wanted to go to England, and told Zen he was at liberty to do the same.

They went to Milan without having patched up their quarrel, but the Milanese Government ordered them to leave Lombardy, and I never heard what arrangements they finally came to. Later on I was informed that the Englishman's bills had all been settled to the uttermost farthing.

Medini, penniless as usual, had taken up his abode in the hotel where I was staying, bringing with him his mistress, her sister, and her mother, but with only one servant. He informed me that the grand duke had refused to listen to any of them at Pisa, where he had received a second order to leave Tuscany, and so had been obliged to sell everything. Of course he wanted me to help him, but I turned a deaf ear to his entreaties.

I have never seen this adventurer without his being in a desperate state of impecuniosity, but he would never learn to abate his luxurious habits, and always managed to find some way or other out of his difficulties. He was lucky enough to fall in with a Franciscan monk named De Dominis at Bologna, the said monk being on his way to Rome to solicit a brief of 'laicisation' from the Pope. He fell in love with Medini's mistress, who naturally made him pay dearly for her charms.

Medini left at the end of three weeks. He went to Germany, where he printed his version of the "Henriade," having discovered a Maecenas in the person of the Elector Palatin. After that he wandered about Europe for twelve years, and died in a London prison in 1788.

I had always warned him to give England a wide berth, as I felt certain that if he once went there he would not escape English bolts and bars, and that if he got on the wrong side of the prison doors he would never come out alive. He despised my advice, and if he did so with the idea of proving me a liar, he made a mistake, for he proved me to be a prophet.

Medini had the advantage of high birth, a good education, and intelligence; but as he was a poor man with luxurious tastes he either corrected fortune at play or went into debt, and was consequently obliged to be always on the wing to avoid imprisonment.

He lived in this way for seventy years, and he might possibly be alive now if he had followed my advice.

Eight years ago Count Torio told me that he had seen Medini in a London prison, and that the silly fellow confessed he had only come to London with the hope of proving me to be a liar.

Medini's fate shall never prevent me from giving good advice to a poor wretch on the brink of the precipice. Twenty years ago I told Cagliostro (who called himself Count Pellegrini in those days) not to set his foot in Rome, and if he had followed this counsel he would not have died miserably in a Roman prison.

Thirty years ago a wise man advised me to beware visiting Spain. I went, but, as the reader knows, I had no reason to congratulate myself on my visit.

A week after my arrival at Bologna, happening to be in the shop of Tartuffi, the bookseller, I made the acquaintance of a cross-eyed priest, who struck me, after a quarter of an hour's talk as a man of learning and talent. He presented me with two works which had recently been issued by two of the young professors at the university He told me that I should find them amusing reading, and he was right.

The first treatise contended that women's faults should be forgiven them, since they were really the work of the matrix, which influenced them in spite of themselves. The second treatise was a criticism of the first. The author allowed that the uterus was an animal, but he denied the alleged influence, as no anatomist had succeeded in discovering any communication between it and the brain.

I determined to write a reply to the two pamphlets, and I did so in the course of three days. When my reply was finished I sent it to M. Dandolo, instructing him to have five hundred copies printed.

When they arrived I gave a bookseller the agency, and in a fortnight I had made a hundred sequins.

The first pamphlet was called "Lutero Pensante," the second was in French and bore the title "La Force Vitale," while I called my reply "Lana Caprina." I treated the matter in an easy vein, not without some hints of deep learning, and made fun of the lucubrations of the two physicians. My preface was in French, but full of Parisian idioms which rendered it unintelligible to all who had not visited the gay capital, and this circumstance gained me a good many friends amongst the younger generation.

The squinting priest, whose name was Zacchierdi, introduced me to the Abbe Severini, who became my intimate friend in the course of ten or twelve days.

This abbe made me leave the inn, and got me two pleasant rooms in the house of a retired artiste, the widow of the tenor Carlani. He also made arrangements with a pastrycook to send me my dinner and supper. All this, plus a servant, only cost me ten sequins a month.

Severini was the agreeable cause of my losing temporarily my taste for study. I put by my "Iliad," feeling sure that I should be able to finish it again.

Severini introduced me to his family, and before long I became very intimate with him. I also became the favourite of his sister, a lady rather plain than pretty, thirty years old, but full of intelligence.

In the course of Lent the abbe introduced me to all the best dancers and operatic singers in Bologna, which is the nursery of the heroines of the stage. They may be had cheaply enough on their native soil.

Every week the good abbe introduced me to a fresh one, and like a true friend he watched carefully over my finances. He was a poor man himself, and could not afford to contribute anything towards the expenses of our little parties; but as they would have cost me double without his help, the arrangement was a convenient one for both of us.

About this time there was a good deal of talk about a Bolognese nobleman, Marquis Albergati Capacelli. He had made a present of his private theatre to the public, and was himself an excellent actor. He had made himself notorious by obtaining a divorce from his wife, whom he did not like, so as to enable him to marry a dancer, by whom he had two children. The amusing point in this divorce was that he obtained it on the plea that he was impotent, and sustained his plea by submitting to an examination, which was conducted as follows:

Four skilled and impartial judges had the marquis stripped before them, and did all in their power to produce an erection; but somehow or other he succeeded in maintaining his composure, and the marriage was pronounced null and void on the ground of relative impotence, for it was well known that he had had children by another woman.

If reason and not prejudice had been consulted, the procedure would have been very different; for if relative impotence was considered a sufficient ground for divorce, of what use was the examination?

The marquis should have sworn that he could do nothing with his wife, and if the lady had traversed this statement the marquis might have challenged her to put him into the required condition.

But the destruction of old customs and old prejudices is often the work of long ages.

I felt curious to know this character, and wrote to M. Dandolo to get me a letter of introduction to the marquis.

In a week my good old friend sent me the desired letter. It was written by another Venetian, M. de Zaguri, an intimate friend of the marquis.

The letter was not sealed, so I read it. I was delighted; no one could have commended a person unknown to himself but the friend of a friend in a more delicate manner.

I thought myself bound to write a letter of thanks to M. Zaguri. I said that I desired to obtain my pardon more than ever after reading his letter, which made me long to go to Venice, and make the acquaintance of such a worthy nobleman.

I did not expect an answer, but I got one. M. Zaguri said that my desire was such a flattering one to himself, that he meant to do his best to obtain my recall.

The reader will see that he was successful, but not till after two years of continuous effort.

Albergati was away from Bologna at the time, but when he returned Severini let me know, and I called at the palace. The porter told me that his excellence (all the nobles are excellences at Bologna) had gone to his country house, where he meant to pass the whole of the spring.

In two or three days I drove out to his villa. I arrived at a charming mansion, and finding no one at the door I went upstairs, and entered a large room where a gentleman and an exceedingly pretty woman were just sitting down to dinner. The dishes had been brought in, and there were only two places laid.

I made a polite bow, and asked the gentleman if I had the honour of addressing the Marquis Albergati. He replied in the affirmative, whereupon I gave him my letter of introduction. He took it, read the superscription, and put it in his pocket, telling me I was very kind to have taken so much trouble, and that he would be sure to read it.

"It has been no trouble at all," I replied, "but I hope you will read the letter. It is written by M. de Zaguri, whom I asked to do me this service, as I have long desired to make your lordship's acquaintance."

His lordship smiled and said very pleasantly that he would read it after dinner, and would see what he could do for his friend Zaguri.

Our dialogue was over in a few seconds. Thinking him extremely rude I turned my back and went downstairs, arriving just in time to prevent the postillion taking out the horses. I promised him a double gratuity if he would take me to some village at hand, where he could bait his horses while I breakfasted.

Just as the postillion had got on horseback a servant came running up. He told me very politely that his excellence begged me to step upstairs.

I put my hand in my pocket and gave the man my card with my name and address, and telling him that that was what his master wanted, I ordered the postillion to drive off at a full gallop.

When we had gone half a league we stopped at a good inn, and then proceeded on our way back to Bologna.

The same day I wrote to M. de Zaguri, and described the welcome I had received at the hands of the marquis. I enclosed the letter in another to M. Dandolo, begging him to read it, and to send it on. I begged the noble Venetian to write to the marquis that having offended me grievously he must prepare to give me due satisfaction.

I laughed with all my heart next day when my landlady gave me a visiting card with the inscription, General the Marquis of Albeygati. She told me the marquis had called on me himself, and on hearing I was out had left his card.

I began to look upon the whole of his proceedings as pure gasconnade, only lacking the wit of the true Gascon. I determined to await M. Zaguri's reply before making up my mind as to the kind of satisfaction I should demand.

While I was inspecting the card, and wondering what right the marquis had to the title of general, Severini came in, and informed me that the marquis had been made a Knight of the Order of St. Stanislas by the King of Poland, who had also given him the style of royal chamberlain.

"Is he a general in the Polish service as well?" I asked.

"I really don't know."

"I understand it all," I said to myself. "In Poland a chamberlain has the rank of adjutant-general, and the marquis calls himself general. But general what? The adjective without a substantive is a mere cheat."

I saw my opportunity, and wrote a comic dialogue, which I had printed the next day. I made a present of the work to a bookseller, and in three or four days he sold out the whole edition at a bajocco apiece.

CHAPTER XIX

Farinello and the Electress Dowager of Saxony—Madame Slopitz—Nina—The Midwife—Madame Soavi—Abbe Bolini—Madame Viscioletta—The Seamstress—The Sorry Pleasure of Revenge—Severini Goes to Naples—My Departure—Marquis Mosca

Anyone who attacks a proud person in a comic vein is almost sure of success; the laugh is generally on his side.

I asked in my dialogue whether it was lawful for a provost-marshal to call himself simply marshal, and whether a lieutenant-colonel had a right to the title of colonel. I also asked whether the man who preferred titles of honour, for which he had paid in hard cash, to his ancient and legitimate rank, could pass for a sage.

Of course the marquis had to laugh at my dialogue, but he was called the general ever after. He had placed the royal arms of Poland over the gate of his palace, much to the amusement of Count Mischinski, the Polish ambassador to Berlin, who happened to be passing through Bologna at that time.

I told the Pole of my dispute with the mad marquis, and persuaded him to pay Albergati a visit, leaving his card. The ambassador did so, and the call was returned, but Albergati's cards no longer bore the title of general.

The Dowager Electress of Saxony having come to Bologna, I hastened to pay my respects to her. She had only come to see the famous castrato Farinello, who had left Madrid, and now lived at Bologna in great comfort. He placed a magnificent collation before the Electress, and sang a song of his own composition, accompanying himself on the piano. The Electress, who was an enthusiastic musician, embraced Farinello, exclaiming,—

"Now I can die happy."

Farinello, who was also known as the Chevalier Borschi had reigned, as it were, in Spain till the Parmese wife of Philip V. had laid plots which obliged him to leave the Court after the disgrace of Enunada. The Electress noticed a portrait of the queen, and spoke very highly of her, mentioning some circumstances which must have taken place in the reign of Ferdinand VI.

The famous musician burst into tears, and said that Queen Barbara was as good as Elizabeth of Parma was wicked.

Borschi might have been seventy when I saw him at Bologna. He was very rich and in the enjoyment of good health, and yet he was unhappy, continually shedding tears at the thought of Spain.

Ambition is a more powerful passion than avarice. Besides, Farinello had another reason for unhappiness.

He had a nephew who was the heir to all his wealth, whom he married to a noble Tuscan lady, hoping to found a titled family, though in an indirect kind of way. But this marriage was a torment to him, for in his impotent old age he was so unfortunate as to fall in love with his niece, and to become jealous of his nephew. Worse than all the lady grew to hate him, and Farinello had sent his nephew abroad, while he never allowed the wife to go out of his sight.

Lord Lincoln arrived in Bologna with an introduction for the cardinal legate, who asked him to dinner, and did me the honour of giving me an invitation to meet him. The cardinal was thus convinced that Lord Lincoln and I had never met, and that the grand duke of Tuscany had committed a great injustice in banishing me. It was on that occasion that the young nobleman told me how they had spread the snare, though he denied that he had been cheated; he was far too proud to acknowledge such a thing. He died of debauchery in London three or four years after.

I also saw at Bologna the Englishman Aston with Madame Slopitz, sister of the Charming Cailimena. Madame Slopitz was much handsomer than her sister. She had presented Aston with two babes as beautiful as Raphael's cherubs.

I spoke of her sister to her, and from the way in which I sang her praises she guessed that I had loved her. She told me she would be in Florence during the Carnival of 1773, but I did not see her again till the year 1776, when I was at Venice.

The dreadful Nina Bergonci, who had made a madman of Count Ricla, and was the source of all my woes at Barcelona, had come to Bologna at the beginning of Lent, occupying a pleasant house which she had taken. She had carte blanche with a banker, and kept up a great state, affirming herself to be with child by the Viceroy of Catalonia, and demanding the honours which would be given to a queen who had graciously chosen Bologna as the place of her confinement. She had a special recommendation to the legate, who often visited her, but in the greatest secrecy.

The time of her confinement approached, and the insane Ricla sent over a confidential man, Don Martino, who was empowered to have the child baptized, and to recognize it as Ricla's natural offspring.

Nina made a show of her condition, appearing at the theatre and in the public places with an enormous belly. The greatest noble of Bologna paid court to her, and Nina told them that they might do so, but that she could not guarantee their safety from the jealous dagger of Ricla. She was impudent enough to tell them what happened to me at Barcelona, not knowing that I was at Bologna.

She was extremely surprised to hear from Count Zini, who knew me, that I inhabited the same town as herself.

When the count met me he asked me if the Barcelona story was true. I did not care to take him into my confidence, so I replied that I did not know Nina, and that the story had doubtless been made up by her to see whether he would encounter danger for her sake.

When I met the cardinal I told him the whole story, and his eminence was astonished when I gave him some insight into Nina's character, and informed him that she was the daughter of her sister and her grandfather.

"I could stake my life," said I, "that Nina is no more with child than you are."

"Oh, come!" said he, laughing, "that is really too strong; why shouldn't she have a child? It is a very simple matter, it seems to me. Possibly it may not be Ricla's child but there can be no doubt that she is with somebody's child. What object could she have for feigning pregnancy?"

"To make herself famous by defiling the Count de Ricla, who was a model of justice and virtue before knowing this Messalina. If your eminence knew the hideous character of Nina you would not wonder at anything she did."

"Well, we shall see."

"Yes."

About a week later I heard a great noise in the street, and on putting my head out of the window I saw a woman stripped to the waist, and mounted on an ass, being scourged by the hangman, and hooted by a mob of all the biricchini in Bologna. Severini came up at the same moment and informed me that the woman was the chief midwife in Bologna, and that her punishment had been ordered by the cardinal archbishop.

"It must be for some great crime," I observed.

"No doubt. It is the woman who was with Nina the day before yesterday."

"What! has Nina been brought to bed?"

"Yes; but of a still-born child."

"I see it all."

Next day the story was all over the town.

A poor woman had come before the archbishop, and had complained bitterly that the midwife Teresa had seduced her, promising to give her twenty sequins if she would give her a fine boy to whom she had given birth a fortnight ago. She was not given the sum agreed upon, and in her despair at hearing of the death of her child she begged for justice, declaring herself able to prove that the dead child said to be Nina's was in reality her own.

The archbishop ordered his chancellor to enquire into the affair with the utmost secrecy, and then proceed to instant and summary execution.

A week after this scandal Don Martino returned to Barcelona; but Nina remained as impudent as ever, doubled the size of the red cockades which she made her servants wear, and swore that Spain would avenge her on the insolent archbishop. She remained at Bologna six weeks longer, pretending to be still suffering from the effects of her confinement. The cardinal legate, who was ashamed of having had anything to do with such an abandoned prostitute, did his best to have her ordered to leave.

Count Ricla, a dupe to the last, gave her a considerable yearly income on the condition that she should never come to Barcelona again; but in a year the count died.

Nina did not survive him for more than a year, and died miserably from her fearful debauchery. I met her mother and sister at Venice, and she told me the story of the last two years of her daughter's life; but it is so sad and so disgusting a tale that I feel obliged to omit it.

As for the infamous midwife, she found powerful friends.

A pamphlet appeared in which the anonymous author declared that the archbishop had committed a great wrong in punishing a citizen in so shameful a manner without any of the proper formalities of justice. The writer maintained that even if she were guilty she had been unjustly punished, and should appeal to Rome.

The prelate, feeling the force of these animadversions, circulated a pamphlet in which it appeared that the midwife had made three prior appearances before the judge, and that she would have been sent to the gallows long ago if the archbishop had not hesitated to shame three of the noblest families in Bologna, whose names appeared in documents in the custody of his chancellor.

Her crimes were procuring abortion and killing erring mothers, substituting the living for the dead, and in one case a boy for a girl, thus giving him the enjoyment of property which did not belong to him.

This pamphlet of the prelate reduced the patrons of the infamous midwife to silence, for several young noblemen whose mothers had been attended by her did not relish the idea of their family secrets being brought to light.

At Bologna I saw Madame Marucci, who had been expelled from Spain for the same reason as Madame Pelliccia. The latter had retired to Rome, while Madame Marucci was on her way to Lucca, her native country.

Madame Soavi, a Bolognese dancer whom I had known at Parma and Paris, came to Bologna with her daughter by M. de Marigni. The girl, whose name was Adelaide, was very beautiful, and her natural abilities had been fostered by a careful education.

When Madame Soavi got to Bologna she met her husband whom she had not seen for fifteen years.

"Here is a treasure for you," said she, shewing him her daughter.

"She's certainly very pretty, but what am I to do with her? She does not belong to me."

"Yes she does, as I have given her to you. You must know that she has six thousand francs a year, and that I shall be her cashier till I get her married to a good dancer. I want her to learn character dancing, and to make her appearance on the boards. You must take her out on holidays."

"What shall I say if people ask me who she is?"

"Say she is your daughter, and that you are certain, because your wife gave her to you."

"I can't see that."

"Ah, you have always stayed at home, and consequently your wits are homely."

I heard this curious dialogue which made me laugh then, and makes me laugh now as I write it. I offered to help in Adelaide's education, but Madame Soavi laughed, and said,—

"Fox, you have deceived so many tender pullets, that I don't like to trust you with this one, for fear of your making her too precocious."

"I did not think of that, but you are right."

Adelaide became the wonder of Bologna.

A year after I left the Comte du Barri, brother-in-law of the famous mistress of Louis XV., visited Bologna, and became so amorous of Adelaide that her mother sent her away, fearing he would carry her off.

Du Barri offered her a hundred thousand francs for the girl, but she refused the offer.

I saw Adelaide five years later on the boards of a Venetian theatre. When
I went to congratulate her, she said,—

"My mother brought me into the world, and I think she will send me out of it; this dancing is killing me."

In point of fact this delicate flower faded and died after seven years of the severe life to which her mother had exposed her.

Madame Soavi who had not taken the precaution to settle the six thousand francs on herself, lost all in losing Adelaide, and died miserably after having rolled in riches. But, alas! I am not the man to reproach anyone on the score of imprudence.

At Bologna I met the famous Afflisio, who had been discharged from the imperial service and had turned manager. He went from bad to worse, and five or six years later committed forgery, was sent to the galleys, and there died.

I was also impressed by the example of a man of a good family, who had once been rich. This was Count Filomarino. He was living in great misery, deprived of the use of all his limbs by a succession of venereal complaints. I often went to see him to give him a few pieces of money, and to listen to his malevolent talk, for his tongue was the only member that continued active. He was a scoundrel and a slanderer, and writhed under the thought that he could not go to Naples and torment his relations, who were in reality respectable people, but monsters according to his shewing.

Madame Sabatini, the dancer, had returned to Bologna, having made enough money to rest upon her laurels. She married a professor of anatomy, and brought all her wealth to him as a dower. She had with her her sister, who was not rich and had no talents, but was at the same time very agreeable.

At the house I met an abbe, a fine young man of modest appearance. The sister seemed to be deeply in love with him, while he appeared to be grateful and nothing more.

I made some remark to the modest Adonis, and he gave me a very sensible answer. We walked away together, and after telling each other what brought us to Bologna we parted, agreeing to meet again.

The abbe, who was twenty-four or twenty-five years old, was not in orders, and was the only son of a noble family of Novara, which was unfortunately poor as well as noble.

He had a very scanty revenue, and was able to live more cheaply at Bologna than Novara, where everything is dear. Besides, he did not care for his relations; he had no friends, and everybody there was more or less ignorant.

The Abbe de Bolini, as he was called, was a man of tranquil mind, living a peaceful and quiet life above all things. He liked lettered men more than letters, and did not trouble to gain the reputation of a wit. He knew he was not a fool, and when he mixed with learned men he was quite clever enough to be a good listener.

Both temperament and his purse made him temperate in all things, and he had received a sound Christian education. He never talked about religion, but nothing scandalized him. He seldom praised and never blamed.

He was almost entirely indifferent to women, flying from ugly women and blue stockings, and gratifying the passion of pretty ones more out of kindliness than love, for in his heart he considered women as more likely to make a man miserable than happy. I was especially interested in this last characteristic.

We had been friends for three weeks when I took the liberty of asking him how he reconciled his theories with his attachment to Brigida Sabatini.

He supped with her every evening, and she breakfasted with him every morning. When I went to see him, she was either there already or came in before my call was over. She breathed forth love in every glance, while the abbe was kind, but, in spite of his politeness, evidently bored.

Brigida looked well enough, but she was at least ten years older than the abbe. She was very polite to me and did her best to convince me that the abbe was happy in the possession of her heart, and that they both enjoyed the delights of mutual love.

But when I asked him over a bottle of good wine about his affection for Brigida, he sighed, smiled, blushed, looked down, and finally confessed that this connection was the misfortune of his life.

"Misfortune? Does she make you sigh in vain? If so you should leave her, and thus regain your happiness."

"How can I sigh? I am not in love with her. She is in love with me, and tries to make me her slave."

"How do you mean?"

"She wants me to marry her, and I promised to do so, partly from weakness, and partly from pity; and now she is in a hurry."

"I daresay; all these elderly girls are in a hurry."

"Every evening she treats me to tears, supplications, and despair. She summons me to keep my promise, and accuses me of deceiving her, so you may imagine that my situation is an unhappy one."

"Have you any obligations towards her?"

"None whatever. She has violated me, so to speak, for all the advances came from her. She has only what her sister gives her from day to day, and if she got married she would not get that."

"Have you got her with child?"

"I have taken good care not to do so, and that's what has irritated her; she calls all my little stratagems detestable treason."

"Nevertheless, you have made up your mind to marry her sooner or later?"

"I'd as soon hang myself. If I got married to her I should be four times as poor as I am now, and all my relations at Novara would laugh at me for bringing home a wife of her age. Besides, she is neither rich nor well born, and at Novara they demand the one or the other."

"Then as a man of honour and as a man of sense, you ought to break with her, and the sooner the better."

"I know, but lacking normal strength what am I to do? If I did not go and sup with her to-night, she would infallibly come after me to see what had happened. I can't lock my door in her face, and I can't tell her to go away."

"No, but neither can go on in this miserable way.

"You must make up your mind, and cut the Gordian knot, like Alexander."

"I haven't his sword."

"I will lend it you."

"What do you mean?"

"Listen to me. You must go and live in another town. She will hardly go after you there, I suppose."

"That is a very good plan, but flight is a difficult matter."

"Difficult? Not at all. Do you promise to do what I tell you, and I will arrange everything quite comfortably. Your mistress will not know anything about it till she misses you at supper."

"I will do whatever you tell me, and I shall never forget your kindness; but Brigida will go mad with grief."

"Well my first order to you is not to give her grief a single thought. You have only to leave everything to me. Would you like to start to-morrow?"

"To-morrow?"

"Yes. Have you any debts?"

"No."

"Do you want any money?"

"I have sufficient. But the idea of leaving tomorrow has taken my breath away. I must have three days delay."

"Why so?"

"I expect some letters the day after to-morrow, and I must write to my relations to tell them where I am going."

"I will take charge of your letters and send them on to you."

"Where shall I be?"

"I will tell you at the moment of your departure; trust in me. I will send you at once where you will be comfortable. All you have to do is to leave your trunk in the hands of your landlord, with orders not to give it up to anyone but myself."

"Very good. I am to go without my trunk, then."

"Yes. You must dine with me every day till you go, and mind not to tell anyone whatsoever that you intend leaving Bologna."

"I will take care not to do so."

The worthy young fellow looked quite radiant. I embraced him and thanked him for putting so much trust in me.

I felt proud at the good work I was about to perform, and smiled at the thought of Brigida's anger when she found that her lover had escaped. I wrote to my good friend Dandolo that in five or six days a young abbe would present himself before him bearing a letter from myself. I begged Dandolo to get him a comfortable and cheap lodging, as my friend was so unfortunate as to be indifferently provided with money, though an excellent man. I then wrote the letter of which the abbe was to be the bearer.

Next day Bolini told me that Brigida was far from suspecting his flight, as owing to his gaiety at the thought of freedom he had contented her so well during the night she had passed with him that she thought him as much in love as she was.

"She has all my linen," he added, "but I hope to get a good part of it back under one pretext or another, and she is welcome to the rest."

On the day appointed he called on me as we had arranged the night before, carrying a huge carpet bag containing necessaries. I took him to Modena in a post chaise, and there we dined; afterward I gave him a letter for M. Dandolo, promising to send on his trunk the next day.

He was delighted to hear that Venice was his destination, as he had long wished to go there, and I promised him that M. Dandolo should see that he lived as comfortably and cheaply as he had done at Bologna.

I saw him off, and returned to Bologna. The trunk I dispatched after him the following day.

As I had expected, the poor victim appeared before me all in tears the next day. I felt it my duty to pity her; it would have been cruel to pretend I did not know the reason for her despair. I gave her a long but kindly sermon, endeavouring to persuade her that I had acted for the best in preventing the abbe marrying her, as such a step would have plunged them both into misery.

The poor woman threw herself weeping at my feet, begging me to bring her abbe back, and swearing by all the saints that she would never mention the word "marriage" again. By way of calming her, I said I would do my best to win him over.

She asked where he was, and I said at Venice; but of course she did not believe me. There are circumstances when a clever man deceives by telling the truth, and such a lie as this must be approved by the most rigorous moralists.

Twenty-seven months later I met Bolini at Venice. I shall describe the meeting in its proper place.

A few days after he had gone, I made the acquaintance of the fair Viscioletta, and fell so ardently in love with her that I had to make up my mind to buy her with hard cash. The time when I could make women fall in love with me was no more, and I had to make up my mind either to do without them or to buy them.

I cannot help laughing when people ask me for advice, as I feel so certain that my advice will not be taken. Man is an animal that has to learn his lesson by hard experience in battling with the storms of life. Thus the world is always in disorder and always ignorant, for those who know are always in an infinitesimal proportion to the whole.

Madame Viscioletta, whom I went to see every day, treated me as the Florentine widow had done, though the widow required forms and ceremonies which I could dispense with in the presence of the fair Viscioletta, who was nothing else than a professional courtezan, though she called herself a virtuosa.

I had besieged her for three weeks without any success, and when I made any attempts she repulsed me laughingly.

Monsignor Buoncompagni, the vice-legate, was her lover in secret, though all the town knew it, but this sort of conventional secrecy is common enough in Italy. As as ecclesiastic he could not court her openly, but the hussy made no mystery whatever of his visits.

Being in need of money, and preferring to get rid of my carriage than of anything else, I announced it for sale at the price of three hundred and fifty Roman crowns. It was a comfortable and handsome carriage, and was well worth the price. I was told that the vice-legate offered three hundred crowns, and I felt a real pleasure in contradicting my favoured rival's desires. I told the man that I had stated my price and meant to adhere to it, as I was not accustomed to bargaining.

I went to see my carriage at noon one day to make sure that it was in good condition, and met the vice-legate who knew me from meeting me at the legate's, and must have been aware that I was poaching on his preserves. He told me rudely that the carriage was not worth more than three hundred crowns, and that I ought to be glad of the opportunity of getting rid of it, as it was much too good for me.

I had the strength of mind to despise his violence, and telling him dryly that I did not chaffer I turned my back on him and went my way.

Next day the fair Viscioletta wrote me a note to the effect that she would be very much obliged if I would let the vice-legate have the carriage at his own price, as she felt sure he would give it to her. I replied that I would call on her in the afternoon, and that my answer would depend on my welcome, I went in due course, and after a lively discussion, she gave way, and I signified my willingness to sell the carriage for the sum offered by the vice-legate.

The next day she had her carriage, and I had my three hundred crowns, and I let the proud prelate understand that I had avenged myself for his rudeness.

About this time Severini succeeded in obtaining a position as tutor in an illustrious Neapolitan family, and as soon as he received his journey-money he left Bologna. I also had thoughts of leaving the town.

I had kept up an interesting correspondence with M. Zaguri, who had made up his mind to obtain my recall in concert with Dandolo, who desired nothing better. Zaguri told me that if I wanted to obtain my pardon I must come and live as near as possible to the Venetian borders, so that the State Inquisitors might satisfy themselves of my good conduct. M. Zuliani, brother to the Duchess of Fiano, gave me the same advice, and promised to use all his interest in my behalf.

With the idea of following this counsel I decided to set up my abode at Trieste, where M. Zaguri told me he had an intimate friend to whom he would give me a letter of introduction. As I could not go by land without passing through the States of Venice I resolved to go to Ancona, whence boats sail to Trieste every day. As I should pass through Pesaro I asked my patron to give me a letter for the Marquis Mosca, a distinguished man of letters whom I had long wished to know. Just then he was a good deal talked about on account of a treatise on alms which he had recently published, and which the Roman curia had placed on the "Index."

The marquis was a devotee as well as a man of learning, and was imbued with the doctrine of St. Augustine, which becomes Jansenism if pushed to an extreme point.

I was sorry to leave Bologna, for I had spent eight pleasant months there. In two days I arrived at Pesaro in perfect health and well provided for in every way.

I left my letter with the marquis, and he came to see me the same day. He said his house would always be open to me, and that he would leave me in his wife's hands to be introduced to everybody and everything in the place. He ended by asking me to dine with him the following day, adding that if I cared to examine his library he could give me an excellent cup of chocolate.

I went, and saw an enormous collection of comments on the Latin poets from Ennius to the poets of the twelfth century of our era. He had had them all printed at his own expense and at his private press, in four tall folios, very accurately printed but without elegance. I told him my opinion, and he agreed that I was right.

The want of elegance which had spared him an outlay of a hundred thousand francs had deprived him of a profit of three hundred thousand.

He presented me with a copy, which he sent to my inn, with an immense folio volume entitled "Marmora Pisaurentia," which I had no time to examine.

I was much pleased with the marchioness, who had three daughters and two sons, all good-looking and well bred.

The marchioness was a woman of the world, while her husband's interests were confined to his books. This difference in disposition sometimes gave rise to a slight element of discord, but a stranger would never have noticed it if he had not been told.

Fifty years ago a wise man said to me: "Every family is troubled by some small tragedy, which should be kept private with the greatest care. In fine, people should learn to wash their dirty linen in private."

The marchioness paid me great attention during the five days I spent at Pesaro. In the day she drove me from one country house to another, and at night she introduced me to all the nobility of the town.

The marquis might have been fifty then. He was cold by temperament, had no other passion but that of study, and his morals were pure. He had founded an academy of which he was the president. Its design was a fly, in allusion to his name Mosca, with the words 'de me ce', that is to say, take away 'c' from 'musca' and you have 'musa'.

His only failing was that which the monks regard as his finest quality, he was religious to excess, and this excess of religion went beyond the bounds where 'nequit consistere rectum'.

But which is the better, to go beyond these bounds, or not to come up to them? I cannot venture to decide the question. Horace says,—

"Nulla est mihi religio!"

and it is the beginning of an ode in which he condemns philosophy for estranging him from religion.

Excess of every kind is bad.

I left Pesaro delighted with the good company I had met, and only sorry I had not seen the marquis's brother who was praised by everyone.

CHAPTER XX

A Jew Named Mardocheus Becomes My Travelling Companion—
He Persuades Me to Lodge in His House—I Fall in Love With His
Daughter Leah—After a Stay of Six Weeks I Go to Trieste

Some time elapsed before I had time to examine the Marquis of
Mosca's collection of Latin poets, amongst which the 'Priapeia'
found no place.

No doubt this work bore witness to his love for literature but not to
his learning, for there was nothing of his own in it. All he had
done was to classify each fragment in chronological order. I
should have liked to see notes, comments, explanations, and such
like; but there was nothing of the kind. Besides, the type was not
elegant, the margins were poor, the paper common, and misprints
not infrequent. All these are bad faults, especially in a work
which should have become a classic. Consequently, the book was
not a profitable one; and as the marquis was not a rich man he
was occasionally reproached by his wife for the money he had
expended.

I read his treatise on almsgiving and his apology for it, and
understood a good deal of the marquis's way of thinking. I could
easily imagine that his writings must have given great offence at
Rome, and that with sounder judgment he would have avoided
this danger. Of course the marquis was really in the right, but in
theology one is only in the right when Rome says yes.

The marquis was a rigorist, and though he had a tincture of
Jansenism he often differed from St. Augustine.

He denied, for instance, that almsgiving could annul the penalty attached to sin, and according to him the only sort of almsgiving which had any merit was that prescribed in the Gospel: "Let not thy right hand know what thy left hand doeth."

He even maintained that he who gave alms sinned unless it was done with the greatest secrecy, for alms given in public are sure to be accompanied by vanity.

It might have been objected that the merit of alms lies in the intention with which they are given. It is quite possible for a good man to slip a piece of money into the palm of some miserable being standing in a public place, and yet this may be done solely with the idea of relieving distress without a thought of the onlookers.

As I wanted to go to Trieste, I might have crossed the gulf by a small boat from Pesaro; a good wind was blowing, and I should have got to Trieste in twelve hours. This was my proper way, for I had nothing to do at Ancona, and it was a hundred miles longer; but I had said I would go by Ancona, and I felt obliged to do so.

I had always a strong tincture of superstition, which has exercised considerable influence on my strange career.

Like Socrates I, too, had a demon to whom I referred my doubtful counsels, doing his will, and obeying blindly when I felt a voice within me telling me to forbear.

A hundred times have I thus followed my genius, and occasionally I have felt inclined to complain that it did not impel me to act against my reason more frequently. Whenever I did so I found that impulse was right and reason wrong, and for all that I have still continued reasoning.

When I arrived at Senegallia, at three stages from Ancona, my vetturino asked me, just as I was going to bed, whether I would allow him to accommodate a Jew who was going to Ancona in the chaise.

My first impulse made me answer sharply that I wanted no one in my chaise, much less a Jew.

The vetturino went out, but a voice said within me, "You must take this' poor Israelite;" and in spite of my repugnance I called back the man and signified my assent.

"Then you must make up your mind to start at an earlier hour, for it is Friday to-morrow, and you know the Jews are not allowed to travel after sunset."

"I shall not start a moment earlier than I intended, but you can make your horses travel as quickly as you like."

He gave me no answer, and went out. The next morning I found my Jew, an honest-looking fellow, in the carriage. The first thing he asked me was why I did not like Jews.

"Because your religion teaches you to hate men of all other religions, especially Christians, and you think you have done a meritorious action when you have deceived us. You do not look upon us as brothers. You are usurious, unmerciful, our enemies, and so I do not like you."

"You are mistaken, sir. Come with me to our synagogue this evening, and you will hear us pray for all Christians, beginning with our Lord the Pope."

I could not help bursting into a roar of laughter.

"True," I replied, "but the prayer comes from the mouth only, and not from the heart. If you do not immediately confess that the Jews would not pray for the Christians if they were the masters, I will fling you out of the chaise."

Of course I did not carry out this threat, but I completed his confusion by quoting in Hebrew the passages in the Old Testament, where the Jews are bidden to do all possible harm to the Gentiles, whom they were to curse every day.

After this the poor man said no more. When we were going to take our dinner I asked him to sit beside me, but he said his religion would not allow him to do so, and that he would only eat eggs, fruit, and some foiegras sausage he had in his pocket. He only drank water because he was not sure that the wine was unadulterated.

"You stupid fellow," I exclaimed, "how can you ever be certain of the purity of wine unless you have made it yourself?"

When we were on our way again he said that if I liked to come and stay with him, and to content myself with such dishes as God had not forbidden, he would make me more comfortable than if I went to the inn, and at a cheaper rate.

"Then you let lodgings to Christians?"

"I don't let lodgings to anybody, but I will make an exception in your case to disabuse you of some of your mistaken notions. I will only ask you six pauls a day, and give you two good meals without wine."

"Then you must give me fish and wine, I paying for them as extras."

"Certainly; I have a Christian cook, and my wife pays a good deal of attention to the cooking."

"You can give me the foie gras every day, if you will eat it with me."

"I know what you think, but you shall be satisfied."

I got down at the Jew's house, wondering at myself as I did so. However, I knew that if I did not like my accommodation I could leave the next day.

His wife and children were waiting for him, and gave him a joyful welcome in honour of the Sabbath. All servile work was forbidden on this day holy to the Lord; and all over the house, and in the face of all the family, I observed a kind of festal air.

I was welcomed like a brother, and I replied as best I could; but a word from Mardocheus (so he was called) changed their politeness of feeling into a politeness of interest.

Mardocheus shewed me two rooms for me to choose the one which suited me, but liking them both I said I would take the two for another paul a day, with which arrangement he was well enough pleased.

Mardocheus told his wife what we had settled, and she instructed the Christian servant to cook my supper for me.

I had my effects taken upstairs, and then went with Mardocheus to the synagogue.

During the short service the Jews paid no attention to me or to several other Christians who were present. The Jews go to the synagogue to pray, and in this respect I think their conduct worthy of imitation by the Christians.

On leaving the synagogue I went by myself to the Exchange, thinking over the happy time which would never return.

It was in Ancona that I had begun to enjoy life; and when I thought it over, it was quite a shock to find that this was thirty years ago, for thirty years is a long period in a man's life. And yet I felt quite happy, in spite of the tenth lustrum so near at hand for me.

What a difference I found between my youth and my middle age! I could scarcely recognize myself. I was then happy, but now unhappy; then all the world was before me, and the future seemed a gorgeous dream, and now I was obliged to confess that my life had been all in vain. I might live twenty years more, but I felt that the happy time was passed away, and the future seemed all dreary.

I reckoned up my forty-seven years, and saw fortune fly away. This in itself was enough to sadden me, for without the favours of the fickle goddess life was not worth living, for me at all events.

My object, then, was to return to my country; it was as if I struggled to undo all that I had done. All I could hope for was to soften the hardships of the slow but certain passage to the grave.

These are the thoughts of declining years and not of youth. The young man looks only to the present, believes that the sky will always smile upon him, and laughs at philosophy as it vainly preaches of old age, misery, repentance, and, worst of all, abhorred death.

Such were my thoughts twenty-six years ago; what must they be now, when I am all alone, poor, despised, and impotent. They would kill me if I did not resolutely subdue them, for whether for good or ill my heart is still young. Of what use are desires when one can no longer satisfy them? I write to kill ennui, and I take a pleasure in writing. Whether I write sense or nonsense, what matters? I am amused, and that is enough.

'Malo scriptor delirus, inersque videri,
Dum mea delectent mala me vel denique fallunt,
Quam sapere.'

When I came back I found Mardocheus at supper with his numerous family, composed of eleven or twelve individuals, and including his mother—an old woman of ninety, who looked very well. I noticed another Jew of middle age; he was the husband of his eldest daughter, who did not strike me as pretty; but the younger daughter, who was destined for a Jew of Pesaro, whom she had never seen, engaged all my attention. I remarked to her that if she had not seen her future husband she could not be in love with him, whereupon she replied in a serious voice that it was not necessary to be in love before one married. The old woman praised the girl for this sentiment, and said she had not been in love with her husband till the first child was born.

I shall call the pretty Jewess Leah, as I have good reasons for not using her real name.

While they were enjoying their meal I sat down beside her and tried to make myself as agreeable as possible, but she would not even look at me.

My supper was excellent, and my bed very comfortable.

The next day my landlord told me that I could give my linen to the maid, and that Leah could get it up for me.

I told him I had relished my supper, but that I should like the foie gras every day as I had a dispensation.

"You shall have some to-morrow, but Leah is the only one of us who eats it."

"Then Leah must take it with me, and you can tell her that I shall give her some Cyprus wine which is perfectly pure."

I had no wine, but I went for it the same morning to the Venetian consul, giving him M. Dandolo's letter.

The consul was a Venetian of the old leaven. He had heard my name, and seemed delighted to make my acquaintance. He was a kind of clown without the paint, fond of a joke, a regular gourmand, and a man of great experience. He sold me some Scopolo and old Cyprus Muscat, but he began to exclaim when he heard where I was lodging, and how I had come there.

"He is rich," he said, "but he is also a great usurer, and if you borrow money of him he will make you repent it."

After informing the consul that I should not leave till the end of the month, I went home to dinner, which proved excellent.

The next day I gave out my linen to the maid, and Leah came to ask me how I liked my lace got up.

If Leah had examined me more closely she would have seen that the sight of her magnificent breast, unprotected by any kerchief, had had a remarkable effect on me.

I told her that I left it all to her, and that she could do what she liked with the linen.

"Then it will all come under my hands if you are in no hurry to go."

"You can make me stay as long as you like," said I; but she seemed not to hear this declaration.

"Everything is quite right," I continued, "except the chocolate; I like it well frothed."

"Then I will make it for you myself."

"Then I will give out a double quantity, and we will take it together."

"I don't like chocolate."

"I am sorry to hear that; but you like foie gras?"

"Yes, I do; and from what father tells me I am going to take some with you to-day."

"I shall be delighted."

"I suppose you are afraid of being poisoned?"

"Not at all; I only wish we could die together."

She pretended not to understand, and left me burning with desire. I felt that I must either obtain possession of her or tell her father not to send her into my room any more.

The Turin Jewess had given me some valuable hints as to the conduct of amours with Jewish girls.

My theory was that Leah would be more easily won than she, for at Ancona there was much more liberty than at Turin.

This was a rake's reasoning, but even rakes are mistaken sometimes.

The dinner that was served to me was very good, though cooked in the Jewish style, and Leah brought in the foie gras and sat down opposite to me with a muslin kerchief over her breast.

The foie gras was excellent, and we washed it down with copious libations of Scopolo, which Leah found very much to her taste.

When the foie gras was finished she got up, but I stopped her, for the dinner was only half over.

"I will stay then," said she, "but I am afraid my father will object."

"Very good. Call your master," I said to the maid who came in at that moment, "I have a word to speak to him."

"My dear Mardocheus," I said when he came, "your daughter's appetite doubles mine, and I shall be much obliged if you will allow her to keep me company whenever we have foie gras."

"It isn't to my profit to double your appetite, but if you like to pay double I shall have no objection."

"Very good, that arrangement will suit me."

In evidence of my satisfaction I gave him a bottle of Scopolo, which Leah guaranteed pure.

We dined together, and seeing that the wine was making her mirthful I told her that her eyes were inflaming me and that she must let me kiss them.

"My duty obliges me to say nay. No kissing and no touching; we have only got to eat and drink together, and I shall like it as much as you."

"You are cruel."

"I am wholly dependent on my father."

"Shall I ask your father to give you leave to be kind?"

"I don't think that would be proper, and my father might be offended and not allow me to see you any more."

"And supposing he told you not to be scrupulous about trifles?"

"Then I should despise him and continue to do my duty."

So clear a declaration shewed me that if I persevered in this intrigue I might go on for ever without success. I also bethought me that I ran a risk of neglecting my chief business, which would not allow me to stay long in Ancona.

I said nothing more to Leah just then, and when the dessert came in I gave her some Cyprus wine, which she declared was the most delicious nectar she had ever tasted.

I saw that the wine was heating her, and it seemed incredible to me that Bacchus should reign without Venus; but she had a hard head, her blood was hot and her brain cool.

However, I tried to seize her hand and kiss it, but she drew it away, saying pleasantly,—

"It's too much for honour and too little for love."

This witty remark amused me, and it also let me know that she was not exactly a neophyte.

I determined to postpone matters till the next day, and told her not to get me any supper as I was supping with the Venetian consul.

The consul had told me that he did not dine, but that he would always be delighted to see me at supper.

It was midnight when I came home, and everyone was asleep except the maid who let me in. I gave her such a gratuity that she must have wished me to keep late hours for the rest of my stay.

I proceeded to sound her about Leah, but she told me nothing but good. If she was to be believed, Leah was a good girl, always at work, loved by all, and fancy free. The maid could not have praised her better if she had been paid to do so.

In the morning Leah brought the chocolate and sat down on my bed, saying that we should have some fine foie gras, and that she should have all the better appetite for dinner as she had not taken any supper.

"Why didn't you take any supper?"

"I suppose it was because of your excellent Cyprus wine, to which my father has taken a great liking."

"Ah! he like it? We will give him some."

Leah was in a state of undress as before, and the sight of her half-covered spheres drove me to distraction.

"Are you not aware that you have a beautiful breast?" said I.

"I thought all young girls were just the same."

"Have you no suspicion that the sight is a very pleasant one for me?"

"If that be so, I am very glad, for I have nothing to be ashamed of, for a girl has no call to hide her throat any more than her face, unless she is in grand company."

As she was speaking, Leah looked at a golden heart transfixed with an arrow and set with small diamonds which served me as a shirt stud.

"Do you like the little heart?" said I.

"Very much. Is it pure gold?"

"Certainly, and that being so I think I may offer it to you."

So saying I took it off, but she thanked me politely, and said that a girl who gave nothing must take nothing.

"Take it; I will never ask any favour of you."

"But I should be indebted to you, and that's the reason why I never take anything."

I saw that there was nothing to be done, or rather that it would be necessary to do too much to do anything, and that in any case the best plan would be to give her up.

I put aside all thoughts of violence, which would only anger her or make her laugh at me. I should either have been degraded, or rendered more amorous, and all for nothing. If she had taken offense she would not have come to see me any more, and I should have had nought to complain of. In fine I made up my mind to restrain myself, and indulge no more in amorous talk.

We dined very pleasantly together. The servant brought in some shell-fish, which are forbidden by the Mosaic Law. While the maid was in the room I asked Leah to take some, and she refused indignantly; but directly the girl was gone she took some of her own accord and ate them eagerly, assuring me that it was the first time she had had the pleasure of tasting shellfish.

"This girl," I said to myself, "who breaks the law of her religion with such levity, who likes pleasure and does not conceal it, this is the girl who wants to make me believe that she is insensible to the pleasures of love; that's impossible, though she may not love me. She must have some secret means of satisfying her passions, which in my opinion are very violent. We will see what can be done this evening with the help of a bottle of good Muscat."

However, when the evening came, she said she could not drink or eat anything, as a meal always prevented her sleeping.

The next day she brought me my chocolate, but her beautiful breast was covered with a white kerchief. She sat down on the bed as usual, and I observed in a melancholy manner that she had only covered her breast because I had said I took a pleasure in seeing it.

She replied that she had not thought of anything, and had only put on her kerchief because she had had no time to fasten her stays.

"You are whole right," I said, smilingly, "for if I were to see the whole breast I might not think it beautiful."

She gave no answer, and I finished my chocolate.

I recollected my collection of obscene pictures, and I begged Leah to give me the box, telling her that I would shew her some of the most beautiful breasts in the world.

"I shan't care to see them," said she; but she gave me the box, and sat down on my bed as before.

I took out a picture of a naked woman lying on her back and abusing herself, and covering up the lower part of it I shewed it to Leah.

"But her breast is like any other," said Leah.

"Take away your handkerchief."

"Take it back; it's disgusting. It's well enough done," she added, with a burst of laughter, "but it's no novelty for me."

"No novelty for you?"

"Of course not; every girl does like that before she gets married."

"Then you do it, too?"

"Whenever I want to."

"Do it now."

"A well-bred girl always does it in private."

"And what do you do after?"

"If I am in bed I go to sleep."

"My dear Leah, your sincerity is too much for me. Either be kind or visit me no more."

"You are very weak, I think."

"Yes, because I am strong."

"Then henceforth we shall only meet at dinner. But chew me some more miniatures."

"I have some pictures which you will not like."

"Let me see them."

I gave her Arentin's figures, and was astonished to see how coolly she examined them, passing from one to the other in the most commonplace way.

"Do you think them interesting?" I said.

"Yes, very; they are so natural. But a good girl should not look at such pictures; anyone must be aware that these voluptuous attitudes excite one's emotions."

"I believe you, Leah, and I feel it as much as you. Look here!"

She smiled and took the book away to the window, turning her back towards me without taking any notice of my appeal.

I had to cool down and dress myself, and when the hairdresser arrived
Leah went away, saying she would return me my book at dinner.

I was delighted, thinking I was sure of victory either that day or the next, but I was out of my reckoning.

We dined well and drank better. At dessert Leah took the book out of her pocket and set me all on fire by asking me to explain some of the pictures but forbidding all practical demonstration.

I went out impatiently, determined to wait till next morning.

When the cruel Jewess came in the morning she told me that she wanted explanations, but that I must use the pictures and nothing more as a demonstration of my remarks.

"Certainly," I replied, "but you must answer all my questions as to your sex."

"I promise to do so, if they arise naturally from the pictures."

The lesson lasted two hours, and a hundred times did I curse Aretin and my folly in shewing her his designs, for whenever I made the slightest attempt the pitiless woman threatened to leave me. But the information she gave me about her own sex was a perfect torment to me. She told me the most lascivious details, and explained with the utmost minuteness the different external and internal movements which would be developed in the copulations pictured by Aretin. I thought it quite impossible that she could be reasoning from theory alone. She was not troubled by the slightest tincture of modesty, but philosophized on coition as coolly and much more learnedly than Hedvig. I would willingly have given her all I possessed to crown her science by the performance of the great work. She swore it was all pure theory with her, and I thought she must be speaking the truth when she said she wanted to get married to see if her notions were right or wrong. She looked pensive when I told her that the husband destined for her might be unable to discharge his connubial duties more than once a week.

"Do you mean to say," said she, "that one man is not as good as another?"

"How do you mean?"

"Are not all men able to make love every day, and every hour, just as they eat, drink and sleep every day?"

"No, dear Leah, they that can make love every day are very scarce."

In my state of chronic irritation I felt much annoyed that there was no decent place at Ancona where a man might appease his passions for his money. I trembled to think that I was in danger of falling really in love with Leah, and I told the consul every day that I was in no hurry to go. I was as foolish as a boy in his calf-love. I pictured Leah as the purest of women, for with strong passions she refused to gratify them. I saw in her a model of virtue; she was all self-restraint and purity, resisting temptation in spite of the fire that consumed her.

Before long the reader will discover how very virtuous Leah was.

After nine or ten days I had recourse to violence, not in deeds but in words. She confessed I was in the right, and said my best plan would be to forbid her to come and see me in the morning. At dinner, according to her, there would be no risk.

I made up my mind to ask her to continue her visits, but to cover her breast and avoid all amorous conversation.

"With all my heart," she replied, laughing; "but be sure I shall not be the first to break the conditions."

I felt no inclination to break them either, for three days later I felt weary of the situation, and told the consul I would start on the first opportunity. My passion for Leah was spoiling my appetite, and I thus saw myself deprived of my secondary pleasure without any prospect of gaining my primary enjoyment.

After what I had said to the consul I felt I should be bound to go, and I went to bed calmly enough. But about two o'clock in the morning I had, contrary to my usual habit, to get up and offer sacrifice to Cloacina. I left my room without any candle, as I knew my way well enough about the house.

The temple of the goddess was on the ground floor, but as I had put on my soft slippers, and walked very softly, my footsteps did not make the least noise.

On my way upstairs I saw a light shining through a chink in the door of a room which I knew to be unoccupied. I crept softly up, not dreaming for a moment that Leah could be there at such an hour. But on putting my eye to the chink I found I could see a bed, and on it were Leah and a young man, both stark naked, and occupied in working out Aretin's postures to the best of their ability. They were whispering to one another, and every four or five minutes I had the pleasure of seeing a new posture. These changes of position gave me a view of all the beauties of Leah, and this pleasure was something to set against my rage in having taken such a profligate creature for a virtuous woman.

Every time they approached the completion of the great work they stopped short, and completed what they were doing with their hands.

When they were doing the Straight Tree, to my mind the most lascivious of them all, Leah behaved like a true Lesbian; for while the young man excited her amorous fury she got hold of his instrument and took it between her lips till the work was complete. I could not doubt that she had swallowed the vital fluid of my fortunate rival.

The Adonis then shewed her the feeble instrument, and Leah seemed to regret what she had done. Before long she began to excite him again; but the fellow looked at his watch, pushed her away, and began to put on his shirt.

Leah seemed angry, and I could see that she reproached him for some time before she began to dress.

When they were nearly clothed I softly returned to my room and looked out of a window commanding the house-door. I had not to wait long before I saw the fortunate lover going out.

I went to bed indignant with Leah; I felt myself degraded. She was no longer virtuous, but a villainous prostitute in my eyes; and I fell to sleep with the firm resolve of driving her from my room the next morning, after shaming her with the story of the scene I had witnessed. But, alas, hasty and angry resolves can seldom withstand a few hours' sleep. As soon as I saw Leah coming in with my chocolate, smiling and gay as usual, I told her quite coolly all the exploits I had seen her executing, laying particular stress on the Straight Tree, and the curious liquid she had swallowed. I ended by saying that I hoped she would give me the next night, both to crown my love and insure my secrecy.

She answered with perfect calm that I had nothing to expect from her as she did not love me, and as for keeping the secret she defied me to disclose it.

"I am sure you would not be guilty of such a disgraceful action," said she.

With these words she turned her back on me and went out.

I could not help confessing to myself that she was in the right; I could not bring myself to commit such a baseness. She had made me reasonable in a few words:

"I don't love you." There was no reply to this, and I felt I had no claim on her.

Rather it was she who might complain of me; what right had I to spy over her? I could not accuse her of deceiving me; she was free to do what she liked with herself. My best course was clearly to be silent.

I dressed myself hastily, and went to the Exchange, where I heard that a vessel was sailing for Fiume the same day.

Fiume is just opposite Ancona on the other side of the gulf. From Fiume to Trieste the distance is forty miles, and I decided to go by that route.

I went aboard the ship and took the best place, said good-bye to the consul, paid Mardocheus, and packed my trunks.

Leah heard that I was going the same day, and came and told me that she could not give me back my lace and my silk stockings that day, but that I could have them by the next day.

"Your father," I replied coolly, "will hand them all over to the Venetian consul, who will send them to me at Trieste."

Just as I was sitting down to dinner, the captain of the boat came for my luggage with a sailor. I told him he could have my trunk, and that I would bring the rest aboard whenever he liked to go.

"I intend setting out an hour before dusk."

"I shall be ready."

When Mardocheus heard where I was going he begged me to take charge of a small box and a letter he wanted to send to a friend.

"I shall be delighted to do you this small service."

At dinner Leah sat down with me and chattered as usual, without troubling herself about my monosyllabic answers.

I supposed she wished me to credit her with calm confidence and philosophy, while I looked upon it all as brazen impudence.

I hated and despised her. She had inflamed my passions, told me to my face she did not love me, and seemed to claim my respect through it all. Possibly she expected me to be grateful for her remark that she believed me incapable of betraying her to her father.

As she drank my Scopolo she said there were several bottles left, as well as some Muscat.

"I make you a present of it all," I replied, "it will prime you up for your nocturnal orgies."

She smiled and said I had had a gratuitous sight of a spectacle which was worth money, and that if I were not going so suddenly she would gladly have given me another opportunity.

This piece of impudence made me want to break the wine bottle on her head. She must have known what I was going to do from the way I took it up, but she did not waver for a moment. This coolness of hers prevented my committing a crime.

I contented myself with saying that she was the most impudent slut I had ever met, and I poured the wine into my glass with a shaking hand, as if that were the purpose for which I had taken up the bottle.

After this scene I got up and went into the next room; nevertheless, in half an hour she came to take coffee with me.

This persistence of hers disgusted me, but I calmed myself by the reflection that her conduct must be dictated by vengeance.

"I should like to help you to pack," said she.

"And I should like to be left alone," I replied; and taking her by the arm I led her out of the room and locked the door after her.

We were both of us in the right. Leah had deceived and humiliated me, and I had reason to detest her, while I had discovered her for a monster of hypocrisy and immodesty, and this was good cause for her to dislike me.

Towards evening two sailors came after the rest of the luggage, and thanking my hostess I told Leah to put up my linen, and to give it to her father, who had taken the box of which I was to be the bearer down to the vessel.

We set sail with a fair wind, and I thought never to set face on Leah again. But fate had ordered otherwise.

We had gone twenty miles with a good wind in our quarter, by which we were borne gently from wave to wave, when all of a sudden there fell a dead calm.

These rapid changes are common enough in the Adriatic, especially in the part we were in.

The calm lasted but a short time, and a stiff wind from the west-north-west began to blow, with the result that the sea became very rough, and I was very ill.

At midnight the storm had become dangerous. The captain told me that if we persisted in going in the wind's eye we should be wrecked, and that the only thing to be done was to return to Ancona.

In less than three hours we made the harbour, and the officer of the guard having recognized me kindly allowed me to land.

While I was talking to the officer the sailors took my trunks, and carried them to my old lodgings without waiting to ask my leave.

I was vexed. I wanted to avoid Leah, and I had intended to sleep at the nearest inn. However, there was no help for it. When I arrived the Jew got up, and said he was delighted to see me again.

It was past three o'clock in the morning, and I felt very ill, so I said I would not get up till late, and that I would dine in my bed without any foie gras. I slept ten hours, and when I awoke I felt hungry and rang my bell.

The maid answered and said that she would have the honour of waiting on me, as Leah had a violent headache.

I made no answer, thanking Providence for delivering me from this impudent and dangerous woman.

Having found my dinner rather spare I told the cook to get me a good supper.

The weather was dreadful. The Venetian consul had heard of my return, and not having seen me concluded I was ill, and paid me a two hours' visit. He assured me the storm would last for a week at least. I was very sorry to hear it; in the first place, because I did not want to see any more of Leah, and in the second, because I had not got any money. Luckily I had got valuable effects, so this second consideration did not trouble me much.

As I did not see Leah at supper-time I imagined that she was feigning illness to avoid meeting me, and I felt very much obliged to her on this account. As it appeared, however, I was entirely mistaken in my conjectures.

The next day she came to ask for chocolate in her usual way, but she no longer bore upon her features her old tranquillity of expression.

"I will take coffee, mademoiselle," I observed; "and as I do not want foie gras any longer, I will take dinner by myself. Consequently, you may tell your father that I shall only pay seven pauls a day. In future I shall only drink Orvieto wine."

"You have still four bottles of Scopolo and Cyprus."

"I never take back a present; the wine belongs to you. I shall be obliged by your leaving me alone as much as possible, as your conduct is enough to irritate Socrates, and I am not Socrates. Besides, the very sight of you is disagreeable to me. Your body may be beautiful, but knowing that the soul within is a monster it charms me no longer. You may be very sure that the sailors brought my luggage here without my orders, or else you would never have seen me here again, where I dread being poisoned every day."

Leah went out without giving me any answer, and I felt certain that after my plain-spoken discourse she would take care not to trouble me again.

Experience had taught me that girls like Leah are not uncommon. I had known specimens at Spa, Genoa, London, and at Venice, but this Jewess was the worst I had ever met.

It was Saturday. When Mardocheus came back from the synagogue he asked me gaily why I had mortified his daughter, as she had declared she had done nothing to offend me.

"I have not mortified her, my dear Mardocheus, or at all events, such was not my intention; but as I have put myself on diet, I shall be eating no more foie gras, and consequently I shall dine by myself, and save three pauls a day."

"Leah is quite ready to pay me out of her private purse, and she wants to dine with you to assure you against being poisoned, as she informs me that you have expressed that fear."

"That was only a jest; I am perfectly aware that I am in the house of an honest man. I don't want your daughter to pay for herself, and to prove that I am not actuated by feelings of economy, you shall dine with me too. To offer to pay for me is an impertinence on her part. In fine, I will either dine by myself and pay you seven pawls a day, or I will pay you thirteen, and have both father and daughter to dine with me."

The worthy Mardocheus went away, saying that he really could not allow me to dine by myself.

At dinner-time I talked only to Mardocheus, without glancing at Leah or paying any attention to the witty sallies she uttered to attract me. I only drank Orvieto.

At dessert Leah filled my glass with Scopolo, saying that if I did not drink it neither would she.

I replied, without looking at her, that I advised her only to drink water for the future, and that I wanted nothing at her hands.

Mardocheus, who liked wine, laughed and said I was right, and drank for three.

The weather continued bad, and I spent the rest of the day in writing, and after supper I retired and went to sleep.

Suddenly I was aroused by a slight noise.

"Who is there?" said I.

I heard Leah's voice, whispering in reply,

"'Tis I; I have not come to disturb you, but to justify myself."

So saying she lay down on the bed, but on the outside of the coverlet.

I was pleased with this extraordinary visit, for my sole desire was for vengeance, and I felt certain of being able to resist all her arts. I therefore told her politely enough that I considered her as already justified and that I should be obliged by her leaving me as I wanted to go to sleep.

"Not before you have heard what I have to say."

"Go on; I am listening to you."

Thereupon she began a discourse which I did not interrupt, and which lasted for a good hour.

She spoke very artfully, and after confessing she had done wrong she said that at my age I should have been ready to overlook the follies of a young and passionate girl. According to her it was all weakness, and pardonable at such an age.

"I swear I love you," said she, "and I would have given you good proof before now if I had not been so unfortunate as to love the young Christian you saw with me, while he does not care for me in the least; indeed I have to pay him.

"In spite of my passion," she continued, "I have never given him what a girl can give but once. I had not seen him for six months, and it was your fault that I sent for him, for you inflamed me with your pictures and strong wines."

The end of it all was that I ought to forget everything, and treat her kindly during the few days I was to remain there.

When she finished I did not allow myself to make any objection. I pretended to be convinced, assuring her that I felt I had been in the wrong in letting her see Aretin's figures, and that I would no longer evince any resentment towards her.

As her explanation did not seem likely to end in the way she wished, she went on talking about the weakness of the flesh, the strength of self-love which often hushes the voice of passion, etc., etc.; her aim being to persuade me that she loved me, and that her refusals had all been given with the idea of making my love the stronger.

No doubt I might have given her a great many answers, but I said nothing. I made up my mind to await the assault that I saw was impending, and then by refusing all her advances I reckoned on abasing her to the uttermost. Nevertheless, she made no motion; her hands were at rest, and she kept her face at a due distance from mine.

At last, tired out with the struggle, she left me pretending to be perfectly satisfied with what she had done.

As soon as she had gone, I congratulated myself on the fact that she had confined herself to verbal persuasion; for if she had gone further she would probably have achieved a complete victory, though we were in the dark.

I must mention that before she left me I had to promise to allow her to make my chocolate as usual.

Early the next morning she came for the stick of chocolate. She was in a complete state of negligee, and came in on tiptoe, though if she chose to look towards the bed she might have seen that I was wide awake.

I marked her artifices and her cunning, and resolved to be equal to all her wiles. When she brought the chocolate I noticed that there were two cups on the tray, and I said,—

"Then it is not true that you don't like chocolate?"

"I feel obliged to relieve you of all fear of being poisoned."

I noticed that she was now dressed with the utmost decency, while half an hour before she had only her chemise and petticoat her neck being perfectly bare. The more resolved she seemed to gain the victory, the more firmly I was determined to humiliate her, as it appeared to me the only other alternative would have been my shame and dishonour; and this turned me to stone.

In spite of my resolves, Leah renewed the attack at dinner, for, contrary to my orders, she served a magnificent foie gras, telling me that it was for herself, and that if she were poisoned she would die of pleasure; Mardocheus said he should like to die too, and began regaling himself on it with evident relish.

I could not help laughing, and announced my wish to taste the deadly food, and so we all of us were eating it.

"Your resolves are not strong enough to withstand seduction," said Leah. This remark piqued me, and I answered that she was imprudent to disclose her designs in such a manner, and that she would find my resolves strong enough when the time came.

A faint smile played about her lips.

"Try if you like," I said, "to persuade me to drink some Scopolo or Muscat. I meant to have taken some, but your taunt has turned me to steel. I mean to prove that when I make up my mind I never alter it."

"The strong-minded man never gives way," said Leah, "but the good-hearted man often lets himself be overpersuaded."

"Quite so, and the good-hearted girl refrains from taunting a man for his weakness for her."

I called the maid and told her to go to the Venetian consul's and get me some more Scopolo and Muscat. Leah piqued me once more by saying enthusiastically,—

"I am sure you are the most good-hearted of men as well as the firmest." Mardocheus, who could not make out what we meant, ate, drank, and laughed, and seemed pleased with everything.

In the afternoon I went out to a cafe in spite of the dreadful weather. I thought over Leah and her designs, feeling certain that she would pay me another nocturnal visit and renew the assault in force. I resolved to weaken myself with some common woman, if I could find one at all supportable.

A Greek who had taken me to a disgusting place a few days before, conducted me to another where he introduced me to a painted horror of a woman from whose very sight I fled in terror.

I felt angry that in a town like Ancona a man of some delicacy could not get his money's worth for his money, and went home, supped by myself, and locked the door after me.

The precaution, however, was useless.

A few minutes after I had shut the door, Leah knocked on the pretext that I had forgotten to give her the chocolate.

I opened the door and gave it her, and she begged me not to lock myself in, as she wanted to have an important and final interview.

"You can tell me now what you want to say."

"No, it will take some time, and I should not like to come till everyone is asleep. You have nothing to be afraid of; you are lord of yourself. You can go to bed in peace."

"I have certainly nothing to be afraid of, and to prove it to you I will leave the door open."

I felt more than ever certain of victory, and resolved not to blow out the candles, as my doing so might be interpreted into a confession of fear. Besides, the light would render my triumph and her humiliation more complete. With these thoughts I went to bed.

At eleven o'clock a slight noise told me that my hour had come. I saw Leah enter my room in her chemise and a light petticoat. She locked my door softly, and when I cried, "Well; what do you want with me?" she let her chemise and petticoat drop, and lay down beside me in a state of nature.

I was too much astonished to repulse her.

Leah was sure of victory, and without a word she threw herself upon me, pressing her lips to mine, and depriving me of all my faculties except one.

I utilised a short moment of reflection by concluding that I was a presumptuous fool, and that Leah was a woman with a most extensive knowledge of human nature.

In a second my caress became as ardent as hers, and after kissing her spheres of rose and alabaster I penetrated to the sanctuary of love, which, much to my astonishment, I found to be a virgin citadel.

There was a short silence, and then I said,—

"Dearest Leah, you oblige me to adore you; why did you first inspire me with hate? Are you not come here merely to humiliate me, to obtain an empty victory? If so, I forgive you; but you are in the wrong, for, believe me, enjoyment is sweeter far than vengeance."

"Nay, I have not come to achieve a shameful victory, but to give myself to you without reserve, to render you my conqueror and my king. Prove your love by making me happy, break down the barrier which I kept intact, despite its fragility and my ardour, and if this sacrifice does not convince you of my affection you must be the worst of men."

I had never heard more energetic opinions, and I had never seen a more voluptuous sight. I began the work, and while Leah aided me to the best of her ability, I forced the gate, and on Leah's face I read the most acute pain and pleasure mingled. In the first ecstasy of delight I felt her tremble in every limb.

As for me, my enjoyment was quite new; I was twenty again, but I had the self-restraint of my age, and treated Leah with delicacy, holding her in my arms till three o'clock in the morning. When I left her she was inundated and exhausted with pleasure, while I could do no more.

She left me full of gratitude, carrying the soaking linen away with   her.
I slept on till twelve o'clock.

When I awoke and saw her standing by my bedside with the gentle love of the day after the wedding, the idea of my approaching departure saddened me. I told her so, and she begged me to stay on as long as I could. I repeated that we would arrange everything when we met again at night.

We had a delicious dinner, for Mardocheus was bent on convincing me that he was no miser.

I spent the afternoon with the consul, and arranged that I should go on a Neapolitan man-of-war which was in quarantine at the time, and was to sail for Trieste.

As I should be obliged to pass another month at Ancona, I blessed the storm that had driven me back.

I gave the consul the gold snuff-box with which the Elector of Cologne had presented me, keeping the portrait as a memento. Three days later he handed me forty gold sequins, which was ample for my needs.

My stay in Ancona was costing me dear; but when I told Mardocheus that I should not be going for another month he declared he would no longer feed at my expense. Of course I did not insist. Leah still dined with me.

It has always been my opinion, though perhaps I may be mistaken, that the Jew was perfectly well aware of my relations with his daughter. Jews are usually very liberal on this article, possibly because they count on the child being an Israelite.

I took care that my dear Leah should have no reason to repent of our connection. How grateful and affectionate she was when I told her that I meant to stay another month! How she blessed the bad weather which had driven me back. We slept together every night, not excepting those nights forbidden by the laws of Moses.

I gave her the little gold heart, which might be worth ten sequins, but that would be no reward for the care she had taken of my linen. She also made me accept some splendid Indian handkerchiefs. Six years later I met her again at Pesaro.

I left Ancona on November 14th, and on the 15th I was at Trieste.

CHAPTER XXI

Pittoni—Zaguri—The Procurator Morosini—The Venetian
Consul—Gorice—The French Consul—Madame Leo—My Devotion
to The State Inquisitors—Strasoldo—Madame Cragnoline—
General Burghausen

The landlord asked me my name, we made our agreement, and I
found myself very comfortably lodged. Next day I went to the
post-office and found several letters which had been awaiting me
for the last month. I opened one from M. Dandolo, and found an
open enclosure from the patrician Marco Dona, addressed to Baron
Pittoni, Chief of Police. On reading it, I found I was very warmly
commended to the baron. I hastened to call on him, and gave him
the letter, which he took but did not read. He told me that M.
Donna had written to him about me, and that he would be
delighted to do anything in his power for me.

I then took Mardocheus's letter to his friend Moses Levi. I had not
the slightest idea that the letter had any reference to myself, so I
gave it to the first clerk that I saw in the office.

Levi was an honest and an agreeable man, and the next day he
called on me and offered me his services in the most cordial
manner. He shewed me the letter I had delivered, and I was
delighted to find that it referred to myself. The worthy
Mardocheus begged him to give me a hundred sequins in case I
needed any money, adding that any politeness shewn to me
would be as if shewn to himself.

This behaviour on the part of Mardocheus filled me with gratitude, and reconciled me, so to speak, with the whole Jewish nation. I wrote him a letter of thanks, offering to serve him at Venice in any way I could.

I could not help comparing the cordiality of Levi's welcome with the formal and ceremonious reception of Baron Pittoni. The baron was ten or twelve years younger than I. He was a man of parts, and quite devoid of prejudice. A sworn foe of 'meum and tuum', and wholly incapable of economy, he left the whole care of his house to his valet, who robbed him, but the baron knew it and made no objection. He was a determined bachelor, a gallant, and the friend and patron of libertines. His chief defect was his forgetfulness and absence of mind, which made him mismanage important business.

He was reputed, though wrongly, to be a liar. A liar is a person who tells falsehoods intentionally, while if Pittoni told lies it was because he had forgotten the truth. We became good friends in the course of a month, and we have remained friends to this day.

I wrote to my friends at Venice, announcing my arrival at Trieste, and for the next ten days I kept my room, busied in putting together the notes I had made on Polish events since the death of Elizabeth Petrovna. I meant to write a history of the troubles of unhappy Poland up to its dismemberment, which was taking place at the epoch in which I was writing.

I had foreseen all this when the Polish Diet recognized the dying czarina as Empress of all the Russians, and the Elector of

Brandenburg as King of Prussia, and I proceeded with my history; but only the first three volumes were published, owing to the printers breaking the agreement.

The four last volumes will be found in manuscript after my death, and anyone who likes may publish them. But I have become indifferent to all this as to many other matters since I have seen Folly crowned king of the earth.

To-day there is no such country as Poland, but it might still be in existence if it had not been for the ambition of the Czartoryski family, whose pride had been humiliated by Count Bruhl, the prime minister. To gain vengeance Prince Augustus Czartoryski ruined his country. He was so blinded by passion that he forgot that all actions have their inevitable results.

Czartoryski had determined not only to exclude the House of Saxony from the succession, but to dethrone the member of that family who was reigning. To do this the help of the Czarina and of the Elector of Brandenburg was necessary, so he made the Polish Diet acknowledge the one as Empress of all the Russians, and the other as King of Prussia. The two sovereigns would not treat with the Polish Commonwealth till this claim had been satisfied; but the Commonwealth should never have granted these titles, for Poland itself possessed most of the Russias, and was the true sovereign of Prussia, the Elector of Brandenburg being only Duke of Prussia in reality.

Prince Czartoryski, blinded by the desire of vengeance, persuaded the Diet that to give the two sovereigns these titles would be merely a form, and that they would never become anything more than honorary. This might be so, but if Poland had possessed far-seeing statesmen they would have guessed that an honorary title would end in the usurpation of the whole country.

The Russian palatin had the pleasure of seeing his nephew Stanislas Poniatowski on the throne.

I myself told him that these titles gave a right, and that the promise not to make any use of them was a mere delusion. I added jokingly—for I was obliged to adopt a humorous tone—that before long Europe would take pity on Poland, which had to bear the heavy weight of all the Russias and the kingdom of Prussia as well, and the Commonwealth would find itself relieved of all these charges.

My prophecy has been fulfilled. The two princes whose titles were allowed have torn Poland limb from limb; it is now absorbed in Russia and Prussia.

The second great mistake made by Poland was in not remembering the apologue of the man and the horse when the question of protection presented itself.

The Republic of Rome became mistress of the world by protecting other nations.

Thus Poland came to ruin through ambition, vengeance, and folly—but folly most of all.

The same reason lay at the root of the French Revolution. Louis XVI. paid the penalty of his folly with his life. If he had been a wise ruler he would still be on the throne, and France would have escaped the fury of the Revolutionists. France is sick; in any other country this sickness might be remedied, but I would not wonder if it proved incurable in France.

Certain emotional persons are moved to pity by the emigrant French nobles, but for my part I think them only worthy of contempt. Instead of parading their pride and their disgrace before the eyes of foreign nations, they should have rallied round their king, and either have saved the throne or died under its ruins. What will become of France? It was hard to say; but it is certain that a body without a head cannot live very long, for reason is situate in the head.

On December 1st Baron Pittoni begged me to call on him as some one had come from Venice on purpose to see me.

I dressed myself hastily, and went to the baron's, where I saw a fine-looking man of thirty-five or forty, elegantly dressed. He looked at me with the liveliest interest.

"My heart tells me," I began, "that your excellency's name is Zaguri?"

"Exactly so, my dear Casanova. As soon as my friend Dandolo told me of your arrival here, I determined to come and congratulate you on your approaching recall, which will take place either this year or the next, as I hope to see two friends of mine made Inquisitors. You may judge of my friendship for you when I tell you that I am an 'avogador', and that there is a law forbidding such to leave Venice. We will spend to-day and to-morrow together."

I replied in a manner to convince him that I was sensible of the honour he had done me; and I heard Baron Pittoni begging me to excuse him for not having come to see me. He said he had forgotten all about it, and a handsome old man begged his excellence to ask me to dine with him, though he had not the pleasure of knowing me.

"What!" said Zaguri. "Casanova has been here for the last ten days, and does not know the Venetian consul?"

I hastened to speak.

"It's my own fault," I observed, "I did not like calling on this gentleman, for fear he might think me contraband."

The consul answered wittily that I was not contraband but in quarantine, pending my return to my native land; and that in the meanwhile his house would always be open to me, as had been the house of the Venetian consul at Ancona.

In this manner he let me know that he knew something about me, and I was not at all sorry for it.

Marco Monti, such was the consul's name, was a man of parts and much experience; a pleasant companion and a great conversationalist, fond of telling amusing stories with a grave face—in fact, most excellent company.

I was something of a 'conteur' myself, and we soon became friendly rivals in telling anecdotes. In spite of his thirty additional years I was a tolerable match for him, and when we were in a room there was no question of gaining to kill the time.

We became fast friends, and I benefited a good deal by his offices during the two years I spent in Trieste, and I have always thought that he had a considerable share in obtaining my recall. That was my great object in those days; I was a victim to nostalgia, or home sickness.

With the Swiss and the Sclavs it is really a fatal disease, which carries them off if they are not sent home immediately. Germans are subject to this weakness also; whilst the French suffer very little, and Italians not much more from the complaint.

No rule, however, lacks its exception, and I was one. I daresay I should have got over my nostalgia if I had treated it with contempt, and then I should not have wasted ten years of my life in the bosom of my cruel stepmother Venice.

I dined with M. Zaguri at the consul's, and I was invited to dine with the governor, Count Auersperg, the next day.

The visit from a Venetian 'avogador' made me a person of great consideration. I was no longer looked upon as an exile, but as one who had successfully escaped from illegal confinement.

The day after I accompanied M. Zaguri to Gorice, where he stayed three days to enjoy the hospitality of the nobility. I was included in all their invitations, and I saw that a stranger could live very pleasantly at Gorice.

I met there a certain Count Cobenzl, who may be alive now—a man of wisdom, generosity, and the vastest learning, and yet without any kind of pretention. He gave a State dinner to M. Zaguri, and I had the pleasure of meeting there three or four most charming ladies. I also met Count Tomes, a Spaniard whose father was in in the Austrian service. He had married at sixty, and had five children all as ugly as himself. His daughter was a charming girl in spite of her plainness; she evidently got her character from the mother's side. The eldest son, who was ugly and squinted, was a kind of pleasant madman, but he was also a liar, a profligate, a boaster, and totally devoid of discretion. In spite of these defects he was much sought after in society as he told a good tale and made people laugh. If he had been a student, he would have been a distinguished scholar, as his memory was prodigious. He it was who vainly guaranteed the agreement I made with Valerio Valeri for printing my "History of Poland." I also met at Gorice a Count Coronini, who was known in learned circles as the author of some Latin treatises on diplomacy. Nobody read his books, but everybody agreed that he was a very learned man.

I also met a young man named Morelli, who had written a history of the place and was on the point of publishing the first volume. He gave me his MS. begging me to make any corrections that struck me as desirable. I succeeded in pleasing him, as I gave him back his work without a single note or alteration of any kind, and thus he became my friend.

I became a great friend of Count Francis Charles Coronini, who was a man of talents. He had married a Belgian lady, but not being able to agree they had separated and he passed his time in trifling intrigues, hunting, and reading the papers, literary and political. He laughed at those sages who declared that there was not one really happy person in the world, and he supported his denial by the unanswerable dictum:

"I myself am perfectly happy."

However, as he died of a tumor in the head at the age of thirty-five, he probably acknowledged his mistake in the agonies of death.

There is no such thing as a perfectly happy or perfectly unhappy man in the world. One has more happiness in his life and another more unhappiness, and the same circumstance may produce widely different effects on individuals of different temperaments.

It is not a fact that virtue ensures happiness for the exercise of some virtues implies suffering, and suffering is incompatible with happiness.

My readers may be aware that I am not inclined to make mental pleasure pre-eminent and all sufficing. It may be a fine thing to have a clear conscience, but I cannot see that it would at all relieve the pangs of hunger.

Baron Pittoni and myself escorted Zaguri to the Venetian border, and we then returned to Trieste together.

In three or four days Pittoni took me everywhere, including the club where none but persons of distinction were admitted. This club was held at the inn where I was staying.

Amongst the ladies, the most noteworthy was the wife of the merchant, David Riguelin, who was a Swabian by birth.

Pittoni was in love with her and continued so till her death. His suit lasted for twelve years, and like Petrarch, he still sighed, still hoped, but never succeeded. Her name was Zanetta, and besides her beauty she had the charm of being an exquisite singer and a polished hostess. Still more noteworthy, however, was the unvarying sweetness and equability of her disposition.

I did not want to know her long before recognizing that she was absolutely impregnable. I told Pittoni so, but all in vain; he still fed on empty hope.

Zanetta had very poor health, though no one would have judged so from her appearance, but it was well known to be the case. She died at an early age.

A few days after M. Zaguri's departure, I had a note from the consul informing me that the Procurator Morosini was stopping in my inn, and advising me to call on him if I knew him.

I was infinitely obliged for this advice, for M. Morosini was a personage of the greatest importance. He had known me from childhood, and the reader may remember that he had presented me to Marshal Richelieu, at Fontainebleau, in 1750.

I dressed myself as if I had been about to speak to a monarch, and sent in a note to his room.

I had not long to wait; he came out and welcomed me most graciously, telling me how delighted he was to see me again.

When he heard the reason of my being at Trieste, and how I desired to return to my country, he assured me he would do all in his power to obtain me my wish. He thanked me for the care I had taken of his nephew at Florence, and kept me all the day while I told him my principal adventures.

He was glad to hear that M. Zaguri was working for me, and said that they must concert the mater together. He commended me warmly to the consul, who was delighted to be able to inform the Tribunal of the consideration with which M. Morosini treated me.

After the procurator had gone I began to enjoy life at Trieste, but in strict moderation and with due regard for economy, for I had only fifteen sequins a month. I abjured play altogether.

Every day I dined with one of the circle of my friends, who were the Venetian consul, the French consul (an eccentric but worthy man who kept a good cook), Pittoni, who kept an excellent table, thanks to his man who knew what was to his own interests, and several others.

As for the pleasures of love I enjoyed them in moderation, taking care of my purse and of my health.

Towards the end of the carnival I went to a masked ball at the theatre, and in the course of the evening a harlequin came up and presented his columbine to me. They both began to play tricks on me. I was pleased with the columbine, and felt a strong desire to be acquainted with her. After some vain researches the French consul, M. de St. Sauveur, told me that the harlequin was a young lady of rank, and that the columbine was a handsome young man.

"If you like," he added, "I will introduce you to the harlequin's family, and I am sure you will appreciate her charms when you see her as a girl."

As they persisted in their jokes I was able, without wounding decency overmuch, to convince myself that the consul was right on the question of sex; and when the ball was over I said I should be obliged by his introducing me as he had promised. He promised to do so the day after Ash Wednesday.

Thus I made the acquaintance of Madame Leo, who was still pretty and agreeable, though she had lived very freely in her younger days. There was her husband, a son, and six daughters, all handsome, but especially the harlequin with whom I was much taken. Naturally I fell in love with her, but as I was her senior by thirty years, and had begun my addresses in a tone of fatherly affection, a feeling of shame prevented my disclosing to her the real state of my heart. Four years later she told me herself that she had guessed my real feelings, and had been amused by my foolish restraint.

A young girl learns deeper lessons from nature than we men can acquire with all our experience.

At the Easter of 1773 Count Auersperg, the Governor of Trieste, was recalled to Vienna, and Count Wagensberg took his place. His eldest daughter, the Countess Lantieri, who was a great beauty, inspired me with a passion which would have made me unhappy if I had not succeeded in hiding it under a veil of the profoundest respect.

I celebrated the accession of the new governor by some verses which I had printed, and in which, while lauding the father, I paid conspicuous homage to the charms of the daughter.

My tribute pleased them, and I became an intimate friend of the count's. He placed confidence in me with the idea of my using it to my own advantage, for though he did not say so openly I divined his intention.

The Venetian consul had told me that he had been vainly endeavouring for the last four years to get the Government of Trieste to arrange for the weekly diligence from Trieste to Mestre to pass by Udine, the capital of the Venetian Friuli.

"This alteration," he had said, "would greatly benefit the commerce of the two states; but the Municipal Council of Trieste opposes it for a plausible but ridiculous reason."

These councillors, in the depth of their wisdom, said that if the Venetian Republic desired the alteration it would evidently be to their advantage, and consequently to the disadvantage of Trieste.

The consul assured me that if I could in any way obtain the concession it would weigh strongly in my favour with the State

Inquisitors, and even in the event of my non-success he would represent my exertions in the most favourable light.

I promised I would think the matter over.

Finding myself high in the governor's favour, I took the opportunity of addressing myself to him on the subject. He had heard about the matter, and thought the objection of the Town Council absurd and even monstrous; but he professed his inability to do anything himself.

"Councillor Rizzi," said he, "is the most obstinate of them all, and has led astray the rest with his sophisms. But do you send me in a memorandum shewing that the alteration will have a much better effect on the large commerce of Trieste than on the comparatively trifling trade of Udine. I shall send it into the Council without disclosing the authorship, but backing it with my authority, and challenging the opposition to refute your arguments. Finally, if they do not decide reasonably I shall proclaim before them all my intention to send the memoir to Vienna with my opinion on it."

I felt confident of success, and wrote out a memoir full of incontrovertible reasons in favour of the proposed change.

My arguments gained the victory; the Council were persuaded, and Count Wagensberg handed me the decree, which I immediately laid before the Venetian consul. Following his advice, I wrote to the secretary of the Tribunal to the effect that I was happy to have given the Government a proof of my zeal, and an earnest of my desire to be useful to my country and to be worthy of being recalled.

Out of regard for me the count delayed the promulgation of the decree for a week, so that the people of Udine heard the news from Venice before it had reached Trieste, and everybody thought that the Venetian Government had achieved its ends by bribery. The secretary of the Tribunal did not answer my letter, but he wrote to the consul ordering him to give me a hundred ducats, and to inform me that this present was to encourage me to serve the Republic. He added that I might hope great things from the mercy of the Inquisitors if I succeeded in negotiating the Armenian difficulty.

The consul gave me the requisite information, and my impression was that my efforts would be in vain; however, I resolved to make the attempt.

Four Armenian monks had left the Convent of St. Lazarus at Venice, having found the abbot's tyranny unbearable. They had wealthy relations at Constantinople, and laughed the excommunication of their late tyrant to scorn. They sought asylum at Vienna, promising to make themselves useful to the State by establishing an Armenian press to furnish all the Armenian convents with books. They engaged to sink a capital of a million florins if they were allowed to settle in Austria, to found their press, and to buy or build a convent, where they proposed to live in community but without any abbot.

As might be expected the Austrian Government did not hesitate to grant their request; it did more, it gave them special privileges.

The effect of this arrangement would be to deprive Venice of a lucrative trade, and to place it in the emperor's dominions. Consequently the Viennese Court sent them to Trieste with a strong recommendation to the governor, and they had been there for the past six months.

The Venetian Government, of course, wished to entice them back to Venice. They had vainly induced their late abbot to make handsome offers to them, and they then proceeded by indirect means, endeavoring to stir up obstacles in their way, and to disgust them with Trieste.

The consul told me plainly that he had not touched the matter, thinking success to be out of the question; and he predicted that if I attempted it I should find myself in the dilemma of having to solve the insoluble. I felt the force of the consul's remark when I reflected that I could not rely on the governor's assistance, or even speak to him on the subject. I saw that I must not let him suspect my design, for besides his duty to his Government he was a devoted friend to the interests of Trieste, and for this reason a great patron of the monks.

In spite of these obstacles my nostalgia made me make acquaintance with these monks under pretence of inspecting their Armenian types, which they were already casting. In a week or ten days I became quite intimate with them. One day I said that they were bound in honour to return to the obedience of their abbot, if only to annul his sentence of excommunication.

The most obstinate of them told me that the abbot had behaved more like a despot than a father, and had thus absolved them from their obedience. "Besides," he said, "no rascally priest has any right to cut off good Christians from communion with the Saviour, and we are sure that our patriarch will give us absolution and send us some more monks."

I could make no objection to these arguments; however, I asked on another occasion on what conditions they would return to Venice.

The most sensible of them said that in the first place the abbot must withdraw the four hundred thousand ducats which he had entrusted to the Marquis Serpos at four per cent.

This sum was the capital from which the income of the Convent of St. Lazarus was derived. The abbot had no right whatever to dispose of it, even with the consent of a majority among the monks. If the marquis became bankrupt the convent would be utterly destitute. The marquis was an Armenian diamond merchant, and a great friend of the abbot's.

I then asked the monks what were the other conditions, and they replied that these were some matters of discipline which might easily be settled; they would give me a written statement of their grievances as soon as I could assure them that the Marquis Serpos was no longer in possession of their funds.

I embodied my negotiations in writing, and sent the document to the Inquisitors by the consul. In six weeks I received an answer to the effect that the abbot saw his way to arranging the money difficulty, but that he must see a statement of the reforms demanded before doing so. This decided me to have nothing to do with the affair, but a few words from Count Wagensberg made me throw it up without further delay. He gave me to understand that he knew of my attempts to reconcile the four monks with their abbot, and he told me that he had been sorry to hear the report, as my success would do harm to a country where I lived and where I was treated as a friend.

I immediately told him the whole story, assuring him that I would never have begun the negotiation if I had not been certain of failure, for I heard on undoubted authority that Serpos could not possibly restore the four hundred thousand ducats.

This explanation thoroughly dissipated any cloud that might have arisen between us.

The Armenians bought Councillor Rizzi's house for thirty thousand florins. Here they established themselves, and I visited them from time to time without saying anything more about Venice.

Count Wagensberg gave me another proof of his friendship. Unhappily for me he died during the autumn of the same year, at the age of fifty.

One morning he summoned me, and I found him perusing a document he had just received from Vienna. He told me he was sorry I did not read German, but that he would tell me the contents of the paper.

"Here," he continued, "you will be able to serve your country without in any way injuring Austria.

"I am going to confide in you a State secret (it being understood of course that my name is never to be mentioned) which ought to be greatly to your advantage, whether you succeed or fail; at all hazards your patriotism, your prompt action, and your cleverness in obtaining such information will be made manifest. Remember you must never divulge your sources of information; only tell your Government that you are perfectly sure of the authenticity of the statement you make.

"You must know," he continued, "that all the commodities we export to Lombardy pass through Venice where they have to pay duty. Such has long been the custom, and it may still be so if the Venetian Government will consent to reduce the duty of four per cent to two per cent.

"A plan has been brought before the notice of the Austrian Court, and it has been eagerly accepted. I have received certain orders on the matter, which I shall put into execution without giving any warning to the Venetian Government.

"In future all goods for Lombardy will be embarked here and disembarked at Mezzola without troubling the Republic. Mezzola is in the territories of the Duke of Modem; a ship can cross the gulf in the night, and our goods will be placed in storehouses, which will be erected.

"In this way we shall shorten the journey and decrease the freights, and the Modenese Government will be satisfied with a trifling sum, barely equivalent to a fourth of what we pay to Venice.

"In spite of all this, I feel sure that if the Venetian Government wrote to the Austrian Council of Commerce expressing their willingness to take two per cent henceforth, the proposal would be accepted, for we Austrians dislike novelties.

"I shall not lay the matter before the Town Council for four or five days, as there is no hurry for us; but you had better make haste, that you may be the first to inform your Government of the matter.

"If everything goes as I should wish I hope to receive an order from Vienna suspending the decree just as I am about to make it public."

Next morning the governor was delighted to hear that everything had been finished before midnight. He assured me that the consul should not have official information before Saturday. In the meanwhile the consul's uneasy state of mind was quite a trouble to me, for I could not do anything to set his mind at ease.

Saturday came and Councillor Rizzi told me the news at the club. He seemed in high spirits over it, and said that the loss of Venice was the gain of Trieste. The consul came in just then, and said that the loss would be a mere trifle for Venice, while the first shipwreck would cost more to Trieste than ten years' duty. The consul seemed to enjoy the whole thing, but that was the part he had to play. In all small trading towns like Trieste, people make a great account of trifles.

I went to dine with the consul, who privately confessed his doubts and fears on the matter.

I asked him how the Venetians would parry the blow, and he replied,—

"They will have a number of very learned consultations, and then they will do nothing at all, and the Austrians will send their goods wherever they please."

"But the Government is such a wise one."

"Or rather has the reputation of wisdom."

"Then you think it lives on its reputation?"

"Yes; like all your mouldy institutions, they continue to be simply because they have been. Old Governments are like those ancient dykes which are rotten at the base, and only stay in position by their weight and bulk."

The consul was in the right. He wrote to his chief the same day, and in the course of the next week he heard that their excellencies had received information of the matter some time ago by extraordinary channels.

For the present his duties would be confined to sending in any additional information on the same subject.

"I told you so," said the consul; "now, what do you think of the wisdom of our sages?"

"I think Bedlam of Charenton were their best lodging."

In three weeks the consul received orders to give me another grant of a hundred ducats, and to allow me ten sequins a month, to encourage me to deserve well of the State.

From that time I felt sure I should be allowed to return in the course of the year, but I was mistaken, for I had to wait till the year following.

This new present, and the monthly payment of ten sequins put me at my ease, for I had expensive tastes of which I could not cure myself. I felt pleased at the thought that I was now in the pay of the Tribunal which had punished me, and which I had defied. It seemed to me a triumph, and I determined to do all in my power for the Republic.

Here I must relate an amusing incident, which delighted everyone in
Trieste.

It was in the beginning of summer. I had been eating sardines by the sea-shore, and when I came home at ten o'clock at night I was astonished to be greeted by a girl whom I recognized as Count Strasoldo's maid.

The count was a handsome young man, but poor like most of that name; he was fond of expensive pleasures, and was consequently heavily in debt. He had a small appointment which brought him in an income of six hundred florins, and he had not the slightest difficulty in spending a year's pay in three months. He had agreeable manners and a generous disposition, and I had supped with him in company with Baron Pittoni several times. He had a girl in his service who was exquisitely pretty, but none of the count's friends attempted her as he was very jealous. Like the rest, I had seen and admired her, I had congratulated the count on the possession of such a treasure in her presence, but I had never addressed a word to her.

Strasoldo had just been summoned to Vienna by Count Auersperg who liked him, and had promised to do what he could for him. He had got an employment in Poland, his furniture had been sold, he had taken leave of everyone, and nobody doubted that he would take his pretty maid with him. I thought so too, for I had been to wish him a pleasant journey that morning, and my astonishment at finding the girl in my room may be imagined.

"What do you want, my dear?" I asked.

"Forgive me, sir, but I don't want to go with Strasoldo, and I thought you would protect me. Nobody will be able to guess where I am, and Strasoldo will be obliged to go by himself. You will not be so cruel as to drive me away?"

"No, dearest."

"I promise you I will go away to-morrow, for Strasoldo is going to leave at day-break."

"My lovely Leuzica (this was her name), no one would refuse you an asylum, I least of all. You are safe here, and nobody shall come in without your leave. I am only too happy that you came to me, but if it is true that the count is your lover you may be sure he will not go so easily. He will stay the whole of to-morrow at least, in the hope of finding you again."

"No doubt he will look for me everywhere but here. Will you promise not to make me go with him even if he guesses that I am with you?"

"I swear I will not."

"Then I am satisfied."

"But you will have to share my bed."

"If I shall not inconvenience you, I agree with all my heart."

"You shall see whether you inconvenience me or not. Undress, quick! But where are your things?"

"All that I have is in a small trunk behind the count's carriage, but I don't trouble myself about it."

"The poor count must be raging at this very moment."

"No, for he will not come home till midnight. He is supping with Madame
Bissolotti, who is in love with him."

In the meantime Leuzica had undressed and got into bed. In a moment I was beside her, and after the severe regimen of the last eight months I spent a delicious night in her arms, for of late my pleasures had been few.

Leuzica was a perfect beauty, and worthy to be a king's mistress; and if I had been rich I would have set up a household that I might retain her in my service.

We did not awake till seven o'clock. She got up, and on looking out of the window saw Strasoldo's carriage waiting at the door.

I confronted her by saying that as long as she liked to stay with me no one could force her away.

I was vexed that I had no closet in my room, as I could not hide her from the waiter who would bring us coffee. We accordingly dispensed with breakfast, but I had to find out some way of feeding her. I thought I had plenty of time before me, but I was wrong.

At ten o'clock I saw Strasoldo and his friend Pittoni coming into the inn. They spoke to the landlord, and seemed to be searching the whole place, passing from one room to another.

I laughed, and told Leuzica that they were looking for her, and that our turn would doubtless come before long.

"Remember your promise," said she.

"You may be sure of that."

The tone in which this remark was delivered comforted her, and she exclaimed,—

"Well; well, let them come; they will get nothing by it."

I heard footsteps approaching, and went out, closing the door behind me, and begging them to excuse my not asking them in, as there was a contraband commodity in my room.

"Only tell me that it is not my maid," said Strasoldo, in a pitiable voice. "We are sure she is here, as the sentinel at the gate saw her come in at ten o'clock."

"You are right, the fair Leuzica is at this moment in my room. I have given her my word of honour that no violence shall be used, and you may be sure I shall keep my word."

"I shall certainly not attempt any violence, but I am sure she would come of her own free will if I could speak to her."

"I will ask her if she wishes to see you. Wait a moment."

Leuzica had been listening to our conversation, and when I opened the door she told me that I could let them in.

As soon as Strasoldo appeared she asked him proudly if she was under any obligations to him, if she had stolen anything from him, and if she was not perfectly free to leave him when she liked.

The poor count replied mildly that on the contrary it was he who owed her a year's wages and had her box in his possession, but that she should not have left him without giving any reason.

"The only reason is that I don't want to go to Vienna," she replied. "I told you so a week ago. If you are an honest man you will leave me my trunk, and as to my wages you can send them to me at my aunt's at Laibach if you haven't got any money now."

I pitied Strasoldo from the bottom of my heart; he prayed and entreated, and finally wept like a child. However, Pittoni roused my choler by saying that I ought to drive the slut out of my room.

"You are not the man to tell me what I ought and what I ought not to do," I replied, "and after I have received her in my apartments you ought to moderate your expressions."

Seeing that I stood on my dignity he laughed, and asked me if I had fallen in love with her in so short a time.

Strasoldo here broke in by saying he was sure she had not slept with me.

"That's where you are mistaken," said she, "for there's only one bed, and I did not sleep on the floor."

They found prayers and reproaches alike useless and left us at noon. Leuzica was profuse in her expressions of gratitude to me.

There was no longer any mystery, so I boldly ordered dinner for two, and promised that she should remain with me till the count had left Trieste.

At three o'clock the Venetian consul came, saying that Count Strasoldo had begged him to use his good offices with me to persuade me to deliver up the fair Leuzica.

"You must speak to the girl herself," I replied; "she came here and stays here of her own free will."

When the worthy man had heard the girl's story he went away, saying that we had the right on our side.

In the evening a porter brought her trunk, and at this she seemed touched but not repentant.

Leuzica supped with me and again shared my couch. The count left Trieste at day-break.

As soon as I was sure that he was gone, I took a carriage and escorted the fair Leuzica two stages on her way to Laibach. We dined together, and I left her in the care of a friend of hers.

Everybody said I had acted properly, and even Pittoni confessed that in my place he would have done the same.

Poor Strasoldo came to a bad end. He got into debt, committed peculation, and had to escape into Turkey and embrace Islam to avoid the penalty of death.

About this time the Venetian general, Palmanova, accompanied by the procurator Erizzo, came to Trieste to visit the governor, Count Wagensberg. In the afternoon the count presented me to the patricians who seemed astonished to see me at Trieste.

The procurator asked me if I amused myself as well as I had done at Paris sixteen years ago, and I told him that sixteen years more, and a hundred thousand francs less, forced me to live in a different fashion. While we were talking, the consul came in to announce that the felucca was ready. Madame de Lantieri as well as her father pressed me to join the party.

I gave a bow, which might mean either no or yes, and asked the consul what the party was. He told me that they were going to see a Venetian man-of-war at anchor in the harbor; his excellence there being the captain I immediately turned to the countess and smilingly professed my regret that I was unable to set foot on Venetian soil.

Everybody exclaimed at me,—

"You have nothing to fear. You are with honest people. Your suspicion is quite offensive."

"That is all very fine, ladies and gentlemen, and I will come with all my heart, if your excellences will assure me that my joining this little party will not be known to the State Inquisitors possibly by to-morrow."

This was enough. Everybody looked at me in silence, and no objections could be found to my argument.

The captain of the vessel, who did not know me, spoke a few whispered words to the others, and then they left.

The next day the consul told me that the captain had praised my prudence in declining to go on board, as if anyone had chanced to tell him my name and my case whilst I was on his ship, it would have been his duty to detain me.

When I told the governor of this remark he replied gravely that he should not have allowed the ship to leave the harbour.

I saw the procurator Erizzo the same evening, and he congratulated me on my discretion, telling me he would take care to let the Tribunal know how I respected its decisions.

About this time I had the pleasure of seeing a beautiful Venetian, who visited Trieste with several of her admirers. She was of the noble family of Bon, and had married Count Romili de Bergamo, who left her free to do whatever she liked. She drew behind her triumphal chariot an old general, Count Bourghausen, a famous rake who had deserted Mars for the past ten years in order to devote his remaining days to the service of Venus. He was a delightful man, and we became friends. Ten years later he was of service to me, as my readers will find in the next volume, which may perhaps be the last.

CHAPTER XXII

Some Adventures at Trieste—I Am of Service to the Venetian Government—My Expedition to Gorice and My Return to Trieste—I Find Irene as an Actress and Expert Gamester

Some of the ladies of Trieste thought they would like to act a French play, and I was made stage manager. I had not only to choose the pieces, but to distribute the parts, the latter being a duty of infinite irksomeness.

All the actresses were new to the boards, and I had immense trouble in hearing them repeat their parts, which they seemed unable to learn by heart. It is a well-known fact that the revolution which is really wanted in Italy is in female education. The very best families with few exceptions are satisfied with shutting up their daughters in a convent for several years till the time comes for them to marry some man whom they never see till the eve or the day of their marriage. As a consequence we have the 'cicisbeo', and in Italy as in France the idea that our nobles are the sons of their nominal fathers is a purely conventional one.

What do girls learn in convents, especially in Italian convents? A few mechanical acts of devotion and outward forms, very little real religion, a good deal of deceit, often profligate habits, a little reading and writing, many useless accomplishments, small music and less drawing, no history, no geography or mythology, hardly any mathematics, and nothing to make a girl a good wife and a good mother.

As for foreign languages, they are unheard of; our own Italian is so soft that any other tongue is hard to acquire, and the 'dolce far niente' habit is an obstacle to all assiduous study.

I write down these truths in spite of my patriotism. I know that if any of my fellow-countrywomen come to read me they will be very angry; but I shall be beyond the reach of all anger.

To return to our theatricals. As I could not make my actresses get their parts letter perfect, I became their prompter, and found out by experience all the ungratefulness of the position.

The actors never acknowledged their debt to the prompter, and put down to his account all the mistakes they make.

A Spanish doctor is almost as badly off; if his patient recovers, the cure is set down to the credit of one saint or another; but if he dies, the physician is blamed for his unskilful treatment.

A handsome negress, who served the prettiest of my actresses to whom I shewed great attentions, said to me one day,—

"I can't make out how you can be so much in love with my mistress, who is as white as the devil."

"Have you never loved a white man?" I asked.

"Yes," said she, "but only because I had no negro, to whom I should certainly have given the preference."

Soon after the negress became mine, and I found out the falsity of the axiom, 'Sublata lucerna nullum discrimen inter feminas', for even in the darkness a man would know a black woman from a white one.

I feel quite sure myself that the negroes are a distinct species from ourselves. There is one essential difference, leaving the colour out of account—namely, that an African woman can either conceive or not, and can conceive a boy or a girl. No doubt my readers will disbelieve this assertion, but their incredulity would cease if I instructed them in the mysterious science of the negresses.

Count Rosenberg, grand chamberlain of the emperor, came on a visit to Trieste in company with an Abbe Casti, whose acquaintance I wished to make on account of some extremely blasphemous poems he had written. However, I was disappointed; and instead of a man of parts, I found the abbe to be an impudent worthless fellow, whose only merit was a knack of versification.

Count Rosenberg took the abbe with him, because he was useful in the capacities of a fool and a pimp-occupations well suited to his morals, though by no means agreeable to his ecclesiastical status. In those days syphilis had not completely destroyed his uvula.

I heard that this shameless profligate, this paltry poetaster, had been named poet to the emperor. What a dishonour to the memory of the great Metastasio, a man free from all vices, adorned with all virtues, and of the most singular ability.

Casti had neither a fine style, nor a knowledge of dramatic requirements, as appears from two or three comic operas composed by him, in which the reader will find nothing but foolish buffooneries badly put together. In one of these comic operas he makes use of slander against King Theodore and the Venetian Republic, which he turns into ridicule by means of pitiful lies.

In another piece called The Cave of Trophonius, Casti made himself the laughing-stock of the literary world by making a display of useless learning which contributes nothing towards the plot.

Among the persons of quality who came to Gorice, I met a certain Count Torriano, who persuaded me to spend the autumn with him at a country house of his six miles from Gorice.

If I had listened to the voice of my good genius I should certainly never have gone.

The count was under thirty, and was not married. He could not exactly be called ugly in spite of his hangdog countenance, in which I saw the outward signs of cruelty, disloyalty, treason, pride, brutal sensuality, hatred, and jealousy. The mixture of bad qualities was such an appalling one that I thought his physiognomy was at fault, and the goods better than the sign. He asked me to come and see him so graciously that I concluded that the man gave the lie to his face.

I asked about him before accepting the invitation, and I heard nothing but good. People certainly said he was fond of the fair sex, and was a fierce avenger of any wrong done to him, but not thinking either of these characteristics unworthy of a gentleman I accepted his invitation. He told me that he would expect me to meet him at Gorice on the first day of September, and that the next day we would leave for his estate.

In consequence of Torriano's invitation I took leave of everybody, especially of Count Wagensberg, who had a serious attack of that malady which yields so easily to mercury when it is administered by a skilled hand, but which kills the unfortunate who falls amongst quacks. Such was the fate of the poor count; he died a month after I had left Trieste.

I left Trieste in the morning, dined at Proseco, and reached Gorice in good time. I called at Count Louis Torriano's mansion, but was told he was out. However, they allowed me to deposit what little luggage I had when I informed them that the count had invited me. I then went to see Count Torres, and stayed with him till supper-time.

When I got back to the count's I was told he was in the country, and would not be back till the next day, and that in the meantime my trunks had been taken to the inn where a room and supper had been ordered.

I was extremely astonished, and went to the inn, where I was served with a bad supper in an uncomfortable room; however, I supposed that the count had been unable to accommodate me in his house, and I excused him though I wished he had forewarned me. I could not understand how a gentleman who has a house and invites a friend can be without a room wherein to lodge him.

Next morning Count Torriano came to see me, thanked me for my punctuality, congratulated himself on the pleasure he expected to derive from my society, and told me he was very sorry we could not start for two days, as a suit was to be heard the next day between himself and a rascally old farmer who was trying to cheat him.

"Well, well," said I, "I will go and hear the pleadings; it will be an amusement for me."

Soon after he took his leave, without asking me where I intended dining, or apologizing for not having accommodated me himself.

I could not make him out; I thought he might have taken offence at my descending at his doors without having given him any warning.

"Come, come, Casanova," I said to myself, "you may be all abroad. Knowledge of character is an unfathomable gulf. We thought we had studied it deeply, but there is still more to learn; we shall see. He may have said nothing out of delicacy. I should be sorry to be found wanting in politeness, though indeed I am puzzled to know what I have done amiss."

I dined by myself, made calls in the afternoon, and supped with Count Tomes. I told him that I promised myself the pleasure of hearing the eloquence of the bar of Gorice the next day.

"I shall be there, too," said he, "as I am curious to see what sort of a face Torriano will put on it, if the countryman wins. I know something about the case," he continued, "and Torriano is sure of victory, unless the documents attesting the farmer's indebtedness happen to be forgeries. On the other hand, the farmer ought to win unless it can be shewn that the receipts signed by Torriano are forgeries. The farmer has lost in the first court and in the second court, but he has paid the costs and appealed from both, though he is a poor man. If he loses to-morrow he will not only be a ruined man, but be sentenced to penal servitude, while if he wins, Torriano should be sent to the galleys, together with his counsel, who has deserved this fate many times before."

I knew Count Tomes passed for somewhat of a scandal-monger, so his remarks made little impression on me beyond whetting my curiosity. The next day I was one of the first to appear in the court, where I found the bench, plaintiff and defendant, and the barristers, already assembled. The farmer's counsel was an old man who looked honest, while the count's had all the impudence of a practised knave. The count sat beside him, smiling disdainfully, as if he was lowering himself to strive with a miserable peasant whom he had already twice vanquished.

The farmer sat by his wife, his son, and two daughters, and had that air of modest assurance which indicates resignation and a good conscience.

I wondered how such honest people could have lost in two courts; I was sure their cause must be a just one.

They were all poorly clad, and from their downcast eyes and their humble looks I guessed them to be the victims of oppression.

Each barrister could speak for two hours.

The farmer's advocate spoke for thirty minutes, which he occupied by putting in the various receipts bearing the count's signature up to the time when he had dismissed the farmer, because he would not prostitute his daughters to him. He then continued, speaking with calm precision, to point out the anachronisms and contradictions in the count's books (which made his client a debtor), and stated that his client was in a position to prosecute the two forgers who had been employed to compass the ruin of an honest family, whose only crime was poverty. He ended his speech by an appeal for costs in all the suits, and for compensation for loss of time and defamation of character.

The harangue of the count's advocate would have lasted more than two hours if the court had not silenced him. He indulged in a torrent of abuse against the other barrister, the experts in hand-writing, and the peasant, whom he threatened with a speedy consignment to the galleys.

The pleadings would have wearied me if I had been a blind man, but as it was I amused myself by a scrutiny of the various physiognomies before me. My host's face remained smiling and impudent through it all.

The pleadings over, the court was cleared, and we awaited the sentence in the adjoining room.

The peasant and his family sat in a corner apart, sad, sorry, and comfortless, with no friend to speak a consoling word, while the count was surrounded by a courtly throng, who assured him that with such a case he could not possibly lose; but that if the judges did deliver judgment against him he should pay the peasant, and force him to prove the alleged forgery.

I listened in profound silence, sympathising with the countryman rather than my host, whom I believed to be a thorough-paced scoundrel, though I took care not to say so.

Count Torres, who was a deadly foe to all prudence and discretion, asked me my opinion of the case, and I whispered that I thought the count should lose, even if he were in the right, on account of the infamous apostrophes of his counsel, who deserved to have his ears cut off or to stand in the pillory for six months.

"And the client too," said Tomes aloud; but nobody had heard what I had said.

After we had waited for an hour the clerk of the court came in with two papers, one of which he gave to the peasant's counsel and the other to Torriano's. Torriano read it to himself, burst into a loud laugh, and then read it aloud.

The court condemned the count to recognize the peasant as his creditor, to pay all costs, and to give him a year's wages as damages; the peasant's right to appeal ad minimum on account of any other complaints he might have being reserved.

The advocate looked downcast, but Torriano consoled him by a fee of six sequins, and everybody went away.

I remained with the defendant, and asked him if he meant to appeal   to Vienna.

"I shall appeal in another sort," said he; but I did not ask him what he meant.

We left Gorice the next morning.

My landlord gave me the bill, and told me he had received instructions not to insist on my paying it if I made any difficulty, as in that case the count would pay himself.

This struck me as somewhat eccentric, but I only laughed. However, the specimens I had seen of his character made me imagine that I was going to spend six weeks with a dangerous original.

In two hours we were at Spessa, and alighted at a large house, with nothing distinguished about it from an architectural point of view. We went up to the count's room, which was tolerably furnished, and after shewing me over the house he took me to my own room. It was on the ground floor, stuffy, dark, and ill furnished.

"Ah!" said he, "this is the room my poor old father used to love to sit in; like you, he was very fond of study. You may be sure of enjoying perfect liberty here, for you will see no one."

We dined late, and consequently no supper was served. The eating and the wine were tolerable, and so was the company of a priest, who held the position of the count's steward; but I was disgusted at hearing the count, who ate ravenously, reproach me with eating too slowly.

When we rose from table he told me he had a lot to do, and that we should see each other the next day.

I went to my room to put things in order, and to get out my papers. I was then working at the second volume of the Polish troubles.

In the evening I asked for a light as it was growing dark, and presently a servant came with one candle. I was indignant; they ought to have given me wax lights or a lamp at least. However, I made no complaint, merely asking one of the servants if I was to rely on the services of any amongst them.

"Our master has given us no instructions on the subject, but of course we will wait on you whenever you call us."

This would have been a troublesome task, as there was no bell, and I should have been obliged to wander all over the house, to search the courtyard, and perhaps the road, whenever I wanted a servant.

"And who will do my room?" I asked.

"The maid."

"Then she has a key of her own?"

"There is no need for a key, as your door has no lock, but you can bolt yourself in at night."

I could only laugh, whether from ill humour or amusement I really cannot say. However, I made no remark to the man.

I began my task, but in half an hour I was so unfortunate as to put out the candle whilst snuffing it. I could not roam about the house in the dark searching for a light, as I did not know my way, so I went to bed in the dark more inclined to swear than to laugh.

Fortunately the bed was a good one, and as I had expected it to be uncomfortable I went to sleep in a more tranquil humour.

In the morning nobody came to attend on me, so I got up, and after putting away my papers I went to say good morning to my host in dressing-gown and nightcap. I found him under the hand of one of his men who served him as a valet. I told him I had slept well, and had come to breakfast with him; but he said he never took breakfast, and asked me, politely enough, not to trouble to come and see him in the morning as he was always engaged with his tenants, who were a pack of thieves. He then added that as I took breakfast he would give orders to the cook to send me up coffee whenever I liked.

"You will also be kind enough to tell your man to give me a touch with his comb after he has done with you."

"I wonder you did not bring a servant."

"If I had guessed that I should be troubling you, I should certainly have brought one."

"It will not trouble me but you, for you will be kept waiting."

"Not at all. Another thing I want is a lock to my door, for I have important papers for which I am responsible, and I cannot lock them up in my trunk whenever I leave my room."

"Everything is safe in my house."

"Of course, but you see how absurd it would be for you to be answerable in case any of my papers were missing. I might be in the greatest distress, and yet I should never tell you of it."

He remained silent for some time, and then ordered his man to tell the priest to put a lock on my door and give me the key.

While he was thinking, I noticed a taper and a book on the table beside his bed. I went up to it, and asked politely if I might see what kind of reading had beguiled him to sleep. He replied as politely, requesting me not to touch it. I withdrew immediately, telling him with a smile that I felt sure that it was a book of prayers, but that I would never reveal his secret.

"You have guessed what it is," he said, laughing.

I left him with a courteous bow, begging him to send me his man and a cup of coffee, chocolate, or broth, it mattered not which.

I went back to my room meditating seriously on his strange behaviour, and especially on the wretched tallow candle which was given me, while he had a wax taper. My first idea was to leave the house immediately, for though I had only fifty ducats in my possession my spirit was as high as when I was a rich man; but on second thoughts I determined not to put myself in the wrong by affronting him in such a signal manner.

The tallow candle was the most grievous wrong, so I resolved to ask the man whether he had not been told to give me wax lights. This was important, as it might be only a piece of knavery or stupidity on the part of the servant.

The man came in an hour with a cup of coffee, sugared according to his taste or that of the cook. This disgusted me, so I let it stay on the table, telling him, with a burst of laughter (if I had not laughed I must have thrown the coffee in his face), that that was not the way to serve breakfast. I then got ready to have my hair done.

I asked him why he had brought me a wretched tallow candle instead of two wax lights.

"Sir," the worthy man replied, humbly, "I could only give you what the priest gave me; I received a wax taper for my master and a candle for you."

I was sorry to have vexed the poor fellow, and said no more, thinking the priest might have taken a fancy to economise for the count's profit or his own. I determined to question him on the subject.

As soon as I was dressed I went out to walk off my bad humour. I met the priest-steward, who had been to the locksmith. He told me that the man had no ready-made locks, but he was going to fit my door with a padlock, of which I should have the key.

"Provided I can lock my door," I said, "I care not how it's done."

I returned to the house to see the padlock fitted, and while the locksmith was hammering away I asked the priest why he had given a tallow candle instead of one or two wax tapers.

"I should never dare to give you tapers, sir, without express orders from the count."

"I should have thought such a thing would go without saying."

"Yes, in other houses, but here nothing goes without saying. I have to buy the tapers and he pays me, and every time he has one it is noted down."

"Then you can give me a pound of wax lights if I pay you for them?"

"Of course, but I think I must tell the count, for you know . . . ."

"Yes, I know all about it, but I don't care."

I gave him the price of a pound of wax lights, and went for a walk, as he told me dinner was at one. I was somewhat astonished on coming back to the house at half-past twelve to be told that the count had been half an hour at table.

I did not know what to make of all these acts of rudeness; however, I moderated my passion once more, and came in remarking that the abbe had told me dinner was at one.

"It is usually," replied the count, "but to-day I wanted to pay some calls and take you with me, so I decided on dining at noon. You will have plenty of time."

He then gave orders for all the dishes that had been taken away to be brought back.

I made no answer, and sat down to table, and feigning good humour ate what was on the table, refusing to touch those dishes which had been taken away. He vainly asked me to try the soup, the beef, the entrees; I told him that I always punished myself thus when I came in late for a nobleman's dinner.

Still dissembling my ill humour, I got into his carriage to accompany him on his round of visits. He took me to Baron del Mestre, who spent the whole of the year in the country with his family, keeping up a good establishment.

The count spent the whole of the day with the baron, putting off the other visits to a future time. In the evening we returned to Spessa. Soon after we arrived the priest returned the money I had given him for the candles, telling me that the count had forgotten to inform him that I was to be treated as himself.

I took this acknowledgement for what it was worth.

Supper was served, and I ate with the appetite of four, while the count hardly ate at all.

The servant who escorted me to my room asked me at what time I should like breakfast. I told him, and he was punctual; and this time the coffee was brought in the coffee-pot and the sugar in the sugar basin.

The valet did my hair, and the maid did my room, everything was changed, and I imagined that I had given the count a little lesson, and that I should have no more trouble with him. Here, however, I was mistaken, as the reader will discover.

Three or four days later the priest came to me one morning, to ask when I would like dinner, as I was to dine in my room.

"Why so?" I asked.

"Because the count left yesterday for Gorice, telling me he did not know when he should come back. He ordered me to give you your meals in your room."

"Very good. I will dine at one."

No one could be more in favour of liberty and independence than myself, but I could not help feeling that my rough host should have told me he was going to Gorice. He stayed a week, and I should have died of weariness if it had not been for my daily visits to the Baron del Mestre. Otherwise there was no company, the priest was an uneducated man, and there were no pretty country girls. I felt as if I could not bear another four weeks of such a doleful exile.

When the count came back, I spoke to him plainly.

"I came to Spessa," I said, "to keep you company and to amuse myself; but I see that I am in the way, so I hope you will take me back to Gorice and leave me there. You must know that I like society as much as you do, and I do not feel inclined to die of solitary weariness in your house."

He assured me that it should not happen again, that he had gone to Gorice to meet an actress, who had come there purposely to see him, and that he had also profited by the opportunity to sign a contract of marriage with a Venetian lady.

These excuses and the apparently polite tone in which they were uttered induced me to prolong my stay with the extraordinary count.

He drew the whole of his income from vineyards, which produced an excellent white wine and a revenue of a thousand sequins a year. However, as the count did his best to spend double that amount, he was rapidly ruining himself. He had a fixed impression that all the tenants robbed him, so whenever he found a bunch of grapes in a cottage he proceeded to beat the occupants unless they could prove that the grapes did not come from his vineyards. The peasants might kneel down and beg pardon, but they were thrashed all the same.

I had been an unwilling witness of several of these arbitrary and cruel actions, when one day I had the pleasure of seeing the count soundly beaten by two peasants. He had struck the first blow himself, but when he found that he was getting the worst of it he prudently took to his heels.

He was much offended with me for remaining a mere spectator of the fray; but I told him very coolly that, being the aggressor, he was in the wrong, and in the second place I was not going to expose myself to be beaten to a jelly by two lusty peasants in another man's quarrel.

These arguments did not satisfy him, and in his rage he dared to tell me that I was a scurvy coward not to know that it was my duty to defend a friend to the death.

In spite of these offensive remarks I merely replied with a glance of contempt, which he doubtless understood.

Before long the whole village had heard what had happened, and the joy was universal, for the count had the singular privilege of being feared by all and loved by none. The two rebellious peasants had taken to their heels. But when it became known that his lordship had announced his resolution to carry pistols with him in all future visits, everybody was alarmed, and two spokesmen were sent to the count informing him that all his tenants would quit the estate in a week's time unless he gave them a promise to leave them in peace in their humble abodes.

The rude eloquence of the two peasants struck me as sublime, but the count pronounced them to be impertinent and ridiculous.

"We have as good a right to taste the vines which we have watered with the sweat of our brow," said they, "as your cook has to taste the dishes before they are served on your table."

The threat of deserting just at the vintage season frightened the count, and he had to give in, and the embassy went its way in high glee at its success.

Next Sunday we went to the chapel to hear mass, and when we came in the priest was at the altar finishing the Credo. The count looked furious, and after mass he took me with him to the sacristy, and begun to abuse and beat the poor priest, in spite of the surplice which he was still wearing. It was really a shocking sight.

The priest spat in his face and cried help, that being the only revenge in his power.

Several persons ran in, so we left the sacristy. I was scandalised, and I told the count that the priest would be certain to go to Udine, and that it might turn out a very awkward business.

"Try to prevent his doing so," I added, "even by violence, but in the first place endeavour to pacify him."

No doubt the count was afraid, for he called out to his servants and ordered them to fetch the priest, whether he could come or no. His order was executed, and the priest was led in, foaming with rage, cursing the count, calling him excommunicated wretch, whose very breath was poisonous; swearing that never another mass should be sung in the chapel that had been polluted with sacrilege, and finally promising that the archbishop should avenge him.

The count let him say on, and then forced him into a chair, and the unworthy ecclesiastic not only ate but got drunk. Thus peace was concluded, and the abbe forgot all his wrongs.

A few days later two Capuchins came to visit him at noon. They did not go, and as he did not care to dismiss them, dinner was served without any place being laid for the friars. Thereupon the bolder of the two informed the count that he had had no dinner. Without replying, the count had him accommodated with a plateful of rice. The Capuchin refused it, saying that he was worthy to sit, not only at his table, but at a monarch's. The count, who happened to be in a good humour, replied that they called themselves "unworthy brethren," and that they were consequently not worthy of any of this world's good things.

The Capuchin made but a poor answer, and as I thought the count to be in the right I proceeded to back him up, telling the friar he ought to be ashamed at having committed the sin of pride, so strictly condemned by the rules of his order.

The Capuchin answered me with a torrent of abuse, so the count ordered a pair of scissors to be brought, that the beards of the filthy rogues might be cut off. At this awful threat the two friars made their escape, and we laughed heartily over the incident.

If all the count's eccentricities had been of this comparatively harmless and amusing nature, I should not have minded, but such was far from being the case.

Instead of chyle his organs must have distilled some virulent poison; he was always at his worst in his after dinner hours. His appetite was furious; he ate more like a tiger than a man. One day we happened to be eating woodcock, and I could not help praising the dish in the style of the true gourmand. He immediately took up his bird, tore it limb from limb, and gravely bade me not to praise the dishes I liked as it irritated him. I felt an inclination to laugh and also an inclination to throw the bottle at his head, which I should probably have indulged in had I been twenty years younger. However, I did neither, feeling that I should either leave him or accommodate myself to his humours.

Three months later Madame Costa, the actress whom he had gone to see at Gorice, told me that she would never have believed in the possibility of such a creature existing if she had not known Count Torriano.

"Though he is a vigorous lover," she continued, "it is a matter of great difficulty with him to obtain the crisis; and the wretched woman in his arms is in imminent danger of being strangled to death if she cannot conceal her amorous ecstacy. He cannot bear to see another's pleasure. I pity his wife most heartily."

I will now relate the incident which put an end to my relations with this venomous creature.

Amidst the idleness and weariness of Spessa I happened to meet a very pretty and very agreeable young widow. I made her some small presents, and finally persuaded her to pass the night in my room. She came at midnight to avoid observation, and left at day-break by a small door which opened on to the road.

We had amused ourselves in this pleasant manner for about a week, when one morning my sweetheart awoke me that I might close the door after her as usual. I had scarcely done so when I heard cries for help. I quickly opened it again, and I saw the scoundrelly Torriano holding the widow with one hand while he beat her furiously with a stick he held in the other. I rushed upon him, and we fell together, while the poor woman made her escape.

I had only my dressing-gown on, and here I was at a disadvantage; for civilized man is a poor creature without his clothes. However, I held the stick with one hand, while I squeezed his throat with the other. On his side he clung to the stick with his right hand, and pulled my hair with the left. At last his tongue started out and he had to let go.

I was on my feet again in an instant, and seizing the stick I aimed a sturdy blow at his head, which, luckily for him, he partially parried.

I did not strike again, so he got up, ran a little way, and began to pick up stones. However, I did not wait to be pelted, but shut myself in my room and lay down on the bed, only sorry that I had not choked the villain outright.

As soon as I had rested I looked to my pistols, dressed myself, and went out with the intention of looking for some kind of conveyance to take me back to Gorice. Without knowing it I took a road that led me to the cottage of the poor widow, whom I found looking calm though sad. She told me she had received most of the blows on her shoulders, and was not much hurt. What vexed her was that the affair would become public, as two peasants had seen the count beating her, and our subsequent combat.

I gave her two sequins, begging her to come and see me at Gorice, and to tell me where I could find a conveyance.

Her sister offered to shew me the way to a farm, where I could get what I wanted. On the way she told me that Torriano had been her sister's enemy before the death of her husband because she rejected all his proposals.

I found a good conveyance at the farm, and the man promised to drive me in to Gorice by dinner-time.

I gave him half-a-crown as an earnest, and went away, telling him to come for me.

I returned to the count's and had scarcely finished getting ready when the conveyance drove up.

I was about to put my luggage in it, when a servant came from the count asking me to give him a moment's conversation.

I wrote a note in French, saying that after what had passed we ought not to meet again under his roof.

A minute later he came into my room, and shut the door, saying,—

"As you won't speak to me, I have come to speak to you."

"What have you got to say?"

"If you leave my house in this fashion you will dishonour me, and I will not allow it."

"Excuse me, but I should very much like to see how you are going to prevent me from leaving your house."

"I will not allow you to go by yourself; we must go together."

"Certainly; I understand you perfectly. Get your sword or your pistols, and we will start directly. There is room for two in the carriage."

"That won't do. You must dine with me, and then we can go in my carriage."

"You make a mistake. I should be a fool if I dined with you when our miserable dispute is all over the village; to-morrow it will have reached Gorice."

"If you won't dine with me, I will dine with you, and people may say what they like. We will go after dinner, so send away that conveyance."

I had to give in to him. The wretched count stayed with me till noon, endeavouring to persuade me that he had a perfect right to beat a country-woman in the road, and that I was altogether in the wrong.

I laughed, and said I wondered how he derived his right to beat a free woman anywhere, and that his pretence that I being her lover had no right to protect her was a monstrous one.

"She had just left my arms," I continued, "was I not therefore her natural protector? Only a coward or a monster like yourself would have remained indifferent, though, indeed, I believe that even you would have done the same."

A few minutes before we sat down to dinner he said that neither of us would profit by the adventure, as he meant the duel to be to the death.

"I don't agree with you as far as I am concerned," I replied; "and as to the duel, you can fight or not fight, as you please; for my part I have had satisfaction. If we come to a duel I hope to leave you in the land of the living, though I shall do my best to lay you up for a considerable time, so that you may have leisure to reflect on your folly. On the other hand, if fortune favours you, you may act as you please."

"We will go into the wood by ourselves, and my coachman shall have orders to drive you wherever you like if you come out of the wood by yourself."

"Very good indeed; and which would you prefer—swords or pistols?"

"Swords, I think."

"Then I promise to unload my pistols as soon as we get into the carriage."

I was astonished to find the usually brutal count become quite polite at the prospect of a duel. I felt perfectly confident myself, as I was sure of flooring him at the first stroke by a peculiar lunge. Then I could escape through Venetian territory where I was not known.

But I had good reasons for supposing that the duel would end in smoke as so many other duels when one of the parties is a coward, and a coward I believed the count to be.

We started after an excellent dinner; the count having no luggage, and mine being strapped behind the carriage.

I took care to draw the charges of my pistols before the count.

I had heard him tell the coachman to drive towards Gorice, but every moment I expected to hear him order the man to drive up this or that turning that we might settle our differences.

I asked no questions, feeling that the initiative lay with him; but we drove on till we were at the gates of Gorice, and I burst out laughing when I heard the count order the coachman to drive to the posting inn.

As soon as we got there he said,—

"You were in the right; we must remain friends. Promise me not to tell anyone of what has happened."

I gave him the promise; we shook hands, and everything was over.

The next day I took up my abode in one of the quietest streets to finish my second volume on the Polish troubles, but I still managed to enjoy myself during my stay at Gorice. At last I resolved on returning to Trieste, where I had more chances of serving and pleasing the State Inquisitors.

I stayed at Gorice till the end of the year 1773, and passed an extremely pleasant six weeks.

My adventure at Spessa had become public property. At first everybody addressed me on the subject, but as I laughed and treated the whole thing as a joke it would soon be forgotten. Torriano took care to be most polite whenever we met; but I had stamped him as a dangerous character, and whenever he asked me to dinner or supper I had other engagements.

During the carnival he married the young lady of whom he had spoken to me, and as long as he lived her life was misery. Fortunately he died a madman thirteen or fourteen years after.

Whilst I was at Gorice Count Charles Coronini contributed greatly to my enjoyment. He died four years later, and a month before his death he sent me his will in ostosyllabic Italian verses—a specimen of philosophic mirth which I still preserve. It is full of jest and wit, though I believe if he had guessed the near approach of death he would not have been so cheerful, for the prospect of imminent destruction can only enliven the heart of a maniac.

During my stay at Gorice a certain M. Richard Lorrain came there. He was a bachelor of forty, who had done good financial service under the Viennese Government, and had now retired with a comfortable pension. He was a fine man, and his agreeable manners and excellent education procured him admission into the best company in the town.

I met him at the house of Count Torres, and soon after he was married to the young countess.

In October the new Council of Ten and the new Inquisitors took office, and my protectors wrote to me that if they could not obtain my pardon in the course of the next twelve months they would be inclined to despair. The first of the Inquisitors was Sagredo, and intimate friend of the Procurator Morosini's; the second, Grimani, the friend of my good Dandolo; and M. Zaguri wrote to me that he would answer for the third, who, according to law, was one of the six councillors who assist the Council of Ten.

It may not be generally known that the Council of Ten is really a council of seventeen, as the Doge has always a right to be present.

I returned to Trieste determined to do my best for the Tribunal, for I longed to return to Venice after nineteen years' wanderings.

I was then forty-nine, and I expected no more of Fortune's gifts, for the deity despises those of ripe age. I thought, however, that I might live comfortably and independently at Venice.

I had talents and experience, I hoped to make use of them, and I thought the Inquisitors would feel bound to give me some sufficient employment.

I was writing the history of the Polish troubles, the first volume was printed, the second was in preparation, and I thought of concluding the work in seven volumes. Afterwards I had a translation of the "Iliad" in view, and other literary projects would no doubt present themselves.

In fine, I thought myself sure of living in Venice, where many persons who would be beggars elsewhere continue to live at their ease.

I left Gorice on the last day of December, 1773, and on January 1st I took up my abode at Trieste.

I could not have received a warmer welcome. Baron Pittoni, the Venetian consul, all the town councillors, and the members of the club, seemed delighted to see me again. My carnival was a pleasant one, and in the beginning of Lent I published the second volume of my work on Poland.

The chief object of interest to me at Trieste was an actress in a company that was playing there. She was no other than the daughter of the so-called Count Rinaldi, and my readers may remember her under the name of Irene. I had loved her at Milan, and neglected her at Genoa on account of her father's misdeeds, and at Avignon I had rescued her at Marcoline's request. Eleven years had passed by since I had heard of her.

I was astonished to see her, and I think more sorry than glad, for she was still beautiful, and I might fall in love again; and being no longer in a position to give her assistance, the issue might be unfortunate for me. However, I called on her the next day, and was greeted with a shriek of delight. She told me she had seen me at the theatre, and felt sure I would come and see her.

She introduced me to her husband, who played parts like Scapin, and to her nine-year-old daughter, who had a talent for dancing.

She gave me an abridged account of her life since we had met. In the year I had seen her at Avignon she had gone to Turin with her father. At Turin she fell in love with her present husband, and left her parents to join her lot to his.

"Since that," she said, "I have heard of my father's death, but I do not know what has become of my mother."

After some further conversation she told me she was a faithful wife, though she did not push fidelity so far as to drive a rich lover to despair.

"I have no lovers here," she added, "but I give little suppers to a few friends. I don't mind the expense, as I win some money at faro."

She was the banker, and she begged me to join the party now and then.

"I will come after the play to-night," I replied, "but you must not expect any high play of me."

I kept the appointment and supped with a number of silly young tradesmen, who were all in love with her.

After supper she held a bank, and I was greatly astonished when I saw her cheating with great dexterity. It made me want to laugh; however, I lost my florins with a good grace and left. However, I did not mean to let Irene think she was duping me, and I went to see her next morning at rehearsal, and complimented her on her dealing. She pretended not to understand what I meant, and on my explaining myself she had the impudence to tell me that I was mistaken.

In my anger I turned my back on her saying, "You will be sorry for this some day."

At this she began to laugh, and said, "Well, well, I confess! and if you tell me how much you lost you shall have it back, and if you like you shall be a partner in the game."

"No, thank you, Irene, I will not be present at any more of your suppers.
But I warn you to be cautious; games of chance are strictly forbidden."

"I know that, but all the young men have promised strict secrecy."

"Come and breakfast with me whenever you like."

A few days later she came, bringing her daughter with her. The girl was pretty, and allowed me to caress her.

One day Baron Pittoni met them at my lodgings, and as he liked young girls as well as I he begged Irene to make her daughter include him in her list of favoured lovers.

I advised her not to reject the offer, and the baron fell in love with her, which was a piece of luck for Irene, as she was accused of playing unlawful games, and would have been severely treated if the baron had not given her warning. When the police pounced on her, they found no gaming and no gamesters, and nothing could be done.

Irene left Trieste at the beginning of Lent with the company to which she belonged. Three years later I saw her again at Padua. Her daughter had become a charming girl, and our acquaintance was renewed in the tenderest manner.

[Thus abruptly end the Memoirs of Giacome Casanova, Chevalier de Seingalt, Knight of the Golden Spur, Prothonotary Apostolic, and Scoundrel Cosmopolitic.]

The End